Never Limit Your Life:

From Personal to Professional

By
Derek W. Clark

Printed in the United States of America.

FIRST EDITION

Never Limit Your Life: From Personal to Professional
WRITTEN BY DEREK W. CLARK

www.NeverLimitYourLife.com and
www.IWillNeverGiveUp.com

CONTACT DEREK CLARK AT
Derek@NeverLimitYourLife.com

Edited by Michael Laemmle
Email: mrlaemmle@gmail.com

PUBLISHED BY NEVER LIMIT YOUR LIFE
OFFERING LIFE COACHING AND SEMINARS
To Book Workshops and Seminars call
1-800-980-0751

www.NeverLimitYourLife.com and
www.IWillNeverGiveUp.com

ISBN 13: 978-0-9825134-2-2

About Derek W. Clark

Derek Clark's story is one of resilience and redemption. While still a toddler, he was the victim of unthinkable physical and mental abuse at the hands of his biological father, who would eventually end up in a prison for the criminally insane. At five years of age, his mother and stepfather turned him over to the California foster care system, where he would spend the next thirteen years of his life, dealing with abandonment issues and overwhelming anxiety. He knows first-hand about coping with adversity and overcoming hardship.

Psychiatric reports state that even at the age of five, Derek had severe behavioral problems and fascination with extreme violence and death. Neurological reports claimed that at six years old, he had the IQ of a two-and-a-half year old. Misdiagnosed with erratic psychosis, Derek was also considered mentally handicapped due to his numerous emotional and language difficulties.

Yet through it all, Derek never gave up, and went from victim to victor. With the help of his foster parents and other mentors, he defied the artificial limitations imposed upon him. His dark past has never held him back from accomplishing whatever he has set his heart and mind to. He is the founder of several successful corporations, a loving husband and father, singer, musician, songwriter, author, and now an international inspirational speaker. He unleashes his creative energy in a never-ending effort to ignite passion in others. His mission is to instill the courage to never lose faith in the quest to become whatever we want to become. His maxim is to make no excuses and never give up.

Author of the *I Will Never Give Up* book series, Derek's true-life trials and personal triumphs have inspired organizations throughout the United States and Canada, who have heard his powerful message of hope and unwavering perseverance. He has been featured on numerous radio shows in many major U.S. cities, newspaper articles, and television programs. He has taken the stage to perform his original music for some

very famous people, including the President
of the United States. He was featured
alongside Lance Armstrong, Michael
Phelps, Johnny Depp, Tyler Perry, Brad Pitt,
Tyra Banks and U2 as "People Who Roar"
by Roar Clothing.

To find out more about Derek Clark and his
inspiring programs, visit
www.IWillNeverGiveUp.com and
www.NeverLimitYourLife.com

CONTENTS

Life Happens 1

Down On the Farm 15

From Personal to Professional 23

What Drives You? 37

Character, Character, Character 49

Be Here Now! 53

Excuses: Fear and Faith 61

Who Do You Surround Yourself
With? 73

I.R.O.C.K. 81

Words and Identity.............................. 95

WILL is the Way 103

Be Valuable to Your Company........ 109

SALES!!! Live Beyond Limits 115

Start Your Own Business?............... 137

Imaginations and Dreams 143

In Summary....................................... 153

Contact/ Keynotes/ Training............ 167

Life Happens

My life has been the ultimate rollercoaster ride: ups, downs, twists and turns. I've thrown my hands up and screamed more times than the kids on Mr. Toad's Wild Ride. Speaking of wild rides, Derek Clark's Wild Ride began before I was even born. My biological father was apparently no peach, even before he came home shell-shocked from his tour as a tank-gunner in World War II. There was also talk that he was brain damaged by an exploding artillery shell in the European theater. He was the type of man who would never seek therapy for his problems. His injury, combined with the mental stresses of war, turned him into an angry man who turned to violence at the drop of a hat.

When my mother became pregnant, my father wasn't pleased by her decision to carry me to term. One drunken day he marched angrily into the diner where she was working and dragged her by the hair through the restaurant into the kitchen. After throwing her hard onto the tile floor, he kicked wildly at her stomach. With no intention of letting up, he was only stopped after being set upon by the staff and pulled away.

Even after this terrible incident, my mother returned to him. She was destitute and desperate, with little education and no marketable skills. Though he was a monstrous man, she found a modicum of economic security by living under his roof. County records indicate that for the next year, my father was savagely abusive to me.

After several years of emotional and physical mistreatment, my mother finally left my biological father for good. He ended up in an institute for the criminally insane after being convicted for a series of armed robberies. I never saw him again. My mother found security in the arms of another man. For me, however, the new family situation was far from redemption.

My stepfather was terribly strict and nearly as volatile as the ogre my mother had left. He was never comfortable raising the child of another man, especially when, as my mother said, I was the spitting image of my real father. She had a great deal of trouble showing me affection herself, given that I was a constant reminder of one of her biggest mistakes. After a few years of troubled home life, my parents literally gave up. When I was five years old they threw me into the jaws of the California foster care system, condemning me to an unknown fate.

Clearly I came from a failing background. I could hardly have known it at the time, but with the right attitude a painful past is nothing more than a series of stepping-stones to a bright future. It wasn't until many years later that I heard this saying: "The bigger your problem, the greater your destiny can be." Extraordinary people have faced extraordinary difficulties. Indeed, if they hadn't, they wouldn't be extraordinary. Whenever you find yourself in a fix, take a moment for a calm assessment of the situation. How can you learn and grow from the circumstances? How can you make use of it? How can you rise above the challenge and overcome it?

Life will test your mettle, and whether you believe it or not, you have the power within you to find victory. The perfect example is Aron Ralston, the young man who cut off his own arm after being pinned down under a rock in a Utah canyon. Why is he such a sought-after speaker and source of inspiration? Because when the chips were down and all hope seemed lost, he found the will to do the unthinkable.

Everybody who has heard his story has asked him or herself, "Could I have done it?" Members of his audience have even been known to pass out at the mere recounting of his harrowing experience. But Ralston didn't commit to the dreaded deed until nearly six days of starvation and dehydration. I think many of us would have found the resolve to do the same thing he did.

The point of life is not to completely avoid trouble, if only because to do so is futile and foolhardy. Suffering is woven into the fabric of life. Even the most seemingly charmed life will not be free of pain. It's what we do with that pain that sets us apart.

The German philosopher Nietzsche once said, "Whatever does not kill me makes me stronger." I think this quote perfectly sums up the proper attitude towards suffering. The hardest steel is tempered in the hottest fires. When we overcome our troubles, the soul becomes more resilient.

Back at what I took to be a warehouse for unwanted children, feeling like I was lost in a wilderness of uncertain perils, I was confronted with a decision. Was I going to let these threatening new circumstances beat me down and destroy my spirit, or was I going to hold my head up and bravely meet any challenges that came hurtling my way? It was the first time I'd been forced to make an important choice of any kind, much less decide what attitude I would carry forth against what I considered a hostile world. But as I found myself backed into a corner, forced to either come out swinging or collapsing in on myself, I decided I must adapt and overcome. Just by deciding this, I found new sources of strength.

This memory of consciously choosing a path of resistance and overcoming has stayed with me all my life, and convinced me that battling successfully with adversity always begins with a choice to be strong. If a scared five year-old boy was able to consciously pull himself up by the bootstraps and show fresh and life-affirming determination, couldn't anybody? Wasn't there some kernel of spirited will power hiding in all of us, waiting to be drawn upon as a source of limitless energy?

In promising not to feel sorry for myself, I avoided getting stuck in the rut of lamenting my fate. Life throws both good and bad at us. Every day may bring us into confrontation with a problem that seems to have no solution, or place us in a situation that plays on our fear of taking action. Yet, obsession about the negative things in our life is like a shovel that digs us inch by inch into a deeper hole. Soon we are in over our heads, and the pit becomes so deep we cannot see the light of day. Fumbling in the dark, we can hardly find the means to climb out of this ditch. But the answer is always there, inside us. Within everyone is the power to lift themselves up into the light.

What, then, is the springboard out of the darkness? The answer is purpose.

What my childhood decision really came down to is that I decided then and there that I must have purpose. Purpose would drive me to overcome the troubles I immediately faced, and the many challenges I sensed were on the horizon. Viktor Frankl, in his book *Man's Search for Meaning*, came to believe that when there is no immediate hope of deliverance, and it seems like there is nothing to live for and no reason to go on, having purpose in one's life is the thing that keeps us going.

Frankl was a Holocaust survivor, and during the years he spent in a Nazi concentration camp, he took note of who survived the ordeal and why. He concluded that the most important thing separating survivors from those who gave in was that each of those who lived had some reason to keep on living. A project they had always wanted to finish, an aspiration that had been denied them since they'd been imprisoned.

Sometimes those who were by all accounts physically weaker survived, simply because there was something in their lives that was left unfinished. Meaning is like a carrot on a stick, dangling in front of us, prodding us to keep going. But unlike the ox that forever chases the carrot, the more effort we exert the closer we come to grasping whatever it is we're chasing. One day, the meaning we seek will be in our very hands.

Purpose wraps us in a protective cloak; it helps defend us from the slings and arrows of fortune. Five year-old boy that I was, I decided my purpose was to be a super hero rock star! That may seem silly, but the idea firmly took root in my mind. I knew I wanted to do big things, make a splash, but always with an idea towards the good. I wanted to do things that put a smile on people's faces, and turned their frowns upside down. But how was I to accomplish this?

Far from on my way to being a rock star, I was a frightened kid at a state holding facility for undesired boys and girls. The place was cold and impersonal, a warehouse or a prison. I could sense the deep anxiety all around me. Some of the children were crying, others lashed out angrily, still others simply sat there, stunned expressions on their faces. There was nobody around to provide comfort or consolation, and we all bore the shame of being unloved. Still, the dream persisted, and I didn't let my harsh environment destroy my aspirations.

For a while I held onto some small hope that my mother would realize she'd made a huge mistake and come running back to get me. As I lay in bed looking up at the ceiling, surrounded by sobbing children, I convinced myself there was no way my mother would dare leave me in such a horrific place. It was like feeding your baby to the dingoes. But there was no rescue—it was not to be. No ensemble of wacky Disney cartoon characters came bursting in to break me out. Mickey wasn't there, or Goofy, or the all-star cast of Toy Story. There was just cement and cinderblock walls, an echoing loneliness, a dull and painful ache in my heart, and strange children weeping all around me. It became clear to me that whatever hope there was must come from within my own heart.

After several days at this holding facility, we were told that we would be placed with temporary foster families. I told myself that this was just the normal course; that there was still plenty of time for the whole family—brother, sister, Mom, and even my stepdad—to appear in the doorway, looking at me with mixed feelings of remorse and renewed commitment to keeping me as their son. But as the day wore on and we were interviewed and evaluated by our caseworkers, it became clear to me that I would have to sell myself to a new family. I was consumed with worry that if my own mother didn't want me, nobody else would either. I would have to buck up though. I figured nobody would want to take a sad, hopeless-looking little boy home. I would have to be all smiles and congeniality.

For the next several months, I went in and out of different foster homes. Sometimes, it seemed they were there to do nothing more than provide a bed to sleep in. I was in rotation as the holding facility became overcrowded, for each new day fresh meat was brought to the grinder. A few families "tried me on" to see if I was a good fit, and I was returned. I guess I was a handful, and not worth the trouble. It looked for a while like nobody would be buying what I was selling.

I never relied on manipulation to get what I wanted, as I was always a straight-up type. Even as a child, I was not afraid to shock you with the truth. I didn't want to pretend to be a kid I wasn't, just to get in good with a family. I wanted people who loved me for who I really was. But that didn't mean I didn't try to put my best foot forward, and come across as somebody worth getting to know. Somebody worth feeding and sheltering, loving and raising.

At long last, the right match was made. One fine Friday, my caseworker drove me out into the countryside for a trial weekend with a new family. We drove out into what I perceived was rural California. I could hardly believe my eyes, and immediately fell in love with the place. For a kid like me, it was a dream come true.

It was a small family farm. There were large fields with tall wild grasses, small orchards with various fruit trees, a large garden, and animals everywhere. Dogs and cats, sure, but also horses, peacocks, rabbits, goats, chickens, and a few happy looking hogs. To me, these were exotic as zoo animals. Their peculiar sounds and rich odors filled the air. There were motorcycles and trucks parked here and there, some being worked on, their parts lying around in piles.

Most interesting of all, there were other kids. Lots of other kids. Six, to be exact. Some were foster kids like me, others were the biological children of the man and woman who owned this place. They all looked like they were having a great time. There was a very different vibe here than the home in which I'd grown up so far, which was always so tense because my stepfather always seemed so angry. Nothing was obsessively cleaned. Nobody was afraid of a little dirt or wear and tear on the furniture. Screen doors slammed shut. Dogs went running in and out of the house. The place

looked used, loved, and lived-in. It looked
like a home.

Down On the Farm

I could never have guessed this farm would be home for the next decade, and these people would become my family. This place and these people would shape my character in ways that would lead to my eventual worldly and business success. What I had going into my farm life experience was a try-anything attitude, a certain devil-may-care approach to risk, and that little sense of purpose I'd formed while at the halfway house. But on this farm I absorbed every major lesson of business success I could have asked for. I think of it as my little MBA Program on the farm. As I milked goats and slopped pigs, I didn't know I was also learning some serious life lessons.

Living on a farm was a lot harder work than I expected. Remember how in the *Karate Kid* movie Mr. Miagi had his protégé Daniel-san painting fences, waxing cars, and a million other tedious chores? Daniel just wanted to learn karate so he could kick butt and protect himself from bullies. He didn't have the foggiest idea he was building the foundations of a master: discipline, thoroughness, and repetition. When Daniel finally confronted Miagi, he was fed up and wanted to know why he hadn't learned anything. Miagi showed him that in fact he'd been learning the whole time. Paint the fence, he said, and as Daniel-san made the motions of brushwork, Miagi threw blows that Daniel-san blocked. He realized he'd been practicing karate all along.

It was this way with me on the farm. I didn't think I was doing anything but backbreaking labor. But in reality I was learning the value of hard work, teamwork, honesty, accountability, responsibility, doing the job the right way, and following through on a task; all traits that would prove invaluable in my professional life.

Humans and animals both relied on me to do my job and do it right. Slacking off was not tolerated, and I've brought this same attitude to every endeavor I've undertaken since. Living on a farm is not all about feeding animals in the pen and eating them on the dinner table. We also had an enormous vegetable garden that needed tending. We harvested corn, tomatoes, green beans, zucchini, squash, and plenty more. My foster parents taught me that if I started crap with people, I was going to shovel crap. Every time I got in trouble for being disrespectful or sent home for fighting, my punishment was to shovel manure. I'd load up buckets and bring them up to the garden.

I won't tell you it was uphill both ways, but it was indeed uphill and a pretty good haul. Often I'd be so angry about shoveling dung I'd defiantly get undressed down to my underwear and go to work. Somewhere there are pictures of me with nothing but a shovel in my hand and a pair of Fruit-o-the-Looms on. From this I learned that even when you're knee-deep in doo-doo, you can cultivate a spirit of resistance, even while managing to do what needs doing.

Milking goats is a chore that is not great fun. It had to be done twice a day, at six in the morning and six at night. When you're just wiping the sleep from your eyes before sunrise, or eager to play with your friends come early evening, the last thing in the world you feel like doing is slipping on rubber boots and squeezing some smelly goat's teats. But there's a long series of steps that must be performed every time, *ad nauseum*. If you don't do it right, you're asking for more hassles piled onto a job you're already none too enthusiastic about.

You have to fill the bucket with just the right amount of grain. You have to separate the goat to be milked, or the others will interfere with your business, even munching on your clothes while you're distracted! Then you have to disinfect the teats, and always be responsive to her movements, even as you use some very particular techniques to work the milk out. You also have to constantly be conscious of your body position, because a kick from a goat is no picnic. Sometimes you're frustrated, but you have to discipline yourself in order to make the milking experience pleasant. If you don't, the goat will remember, and she will make life very difficult for you in the future.

Occasionally I would calmly be milking into a large silver pail when a friend came sauntering by. I'd change the direction of the udder and squirt him right in the face, or get him on the front of the pants so it looked like he peed them. If I wasn't looking for trouble, I'd invite them to bring a mug with some chocolate powder. I'd aim the milk stream right into the cup, and—voila!— warm chocolate milk, just like magic. It was a little goaty, but not too bad. The point is, if you have to commit to a responsibility that's less than engaging, why not have a little fun doing it? Lighten up and the workload becomes lighter too. Stress and anxiety make work become even more boring and tense. If you have a good attitude, things will move quicker and more efficiently.

Teamwork on a farm is crucial to its success. There are many jobs you will fail at completely if you attempt to go it alone. There are also plenty of ways to get injured. I think back to bucking hay bales in particular, which I did with my Dad or older brother. A hay bale can weigh up to 150 pounds, and we had to stack them ten feet high. We used hay bale hooks and synchronized our lift to get each bale neatly placed on top of the pile. You learn to work harmoniously with another person.

You also get a lot of blisters bucking hay; but before long they turn into calluses. I look at this as a kind of metaphor: through repetition of habit, we become more accustomed to whatever task we must accomplish. In much the same way, our bodies and minds become accustomed to certain actions and habits of mind that at first seem unnatural to us. By keeping at it, it becomes second nature.

Honesty and accountability play big roles on a farm. When my father asked me if I fed the horses, slopped the pigs, or collected the chicken eggs, I better have done it. A hungry animal is a grumpy animal, and soon it is a sick and weakened one. If I'd told him I milked the goats when I hadn't, there was a good chance they'd get mastitis, in which the udder swells and puts the goat in miserable pain.

Milking a suffering goat is an awful experience. The goat doesn't want you to touch it, and so kicks wildly and bleats out in agony. You feel guilty because not only did you fail your family and yourself, you failed this poor helpless creature with your negligence. Moreover, when mastitis sets in the milk is no good until the infection clears. You will have to answer to everybody as to why there's no goat milk, and won't you look like a fool!

Responsibility and animal ownership go hand in hand. You have a whole lot of beasts that are not shy about letting you know they're unhappy. Unlike a human being, they won't hold it in. You will hear horses hee-hawing, goats bellowing, and chickens clucking away. And if you're late with the chickens, they will swarm you when you enter their coop, and you'll begin to wonder if you're not in some kind of horror movie.

If the wind is out of control, or the rain and snow is pounding down, you still better get your boots, gloves, and coat on and get out there to take care of business. They're hungry like clockwork. It's slippery, muddy, cold, and wet, and you're going to slip and fall down. Sure, you'd rather be inside with a warm cup of cocoa—but do what needs doing, then you can kick your feet up and direct your time how you will.

I have held many different jobs in many different capacities in my life. I have been the entry-level employee, the boss and company owner, and every position in between. I have worked on a farm, been a delivery driver for a denture company, a respiratory technician, a customer service representative, loan agent, real estate broker, business owner, music producer, author and professional speaker. Every one of these jobs provided me with rewarding challenges, and helped me develop the tools to continually move up the ladder of success.

A varied work experience is invaluable, and has certainly shaped me into the man I am today. I've never worried about getting in the trenches, and knowing a business from the bottom up. The more you know about how a business operates, the more valuable you are to that business. Never worry that a certain job or task is beneath you, or a waste of your time and talent. Anything you undertake is a chance to learn, and these lessons can be incorporated into your over-all vision and knowledge.

From Personal To Professional

Parts of this book are all about me and my life. If you've gotten this far, you already know that. But these are the not the most important sections, not by a long shot. The most important parts of this book are all about YOU. We are going to focus on YOU, the one holding this book in your hands right now. I want YOU to become better and better, until finally you are the best person you can possibly be, personally and professionally. I want YOU to start living beyond your perceived limits. There are no limits, only endless horizons. The future is always bright. The ceiling is glass: it can be broken—so why not smash on through? You were meant to follow your dreams, and follow through on achieving those dreams.

Professional success always begins with personal success. Take care of yourself, and the rest will follow in tow. A very successful businessman friend of mine was once asked for his opinion on the first rule of success.

He replied: "Character, character, character." Notice how he didn't say, greed-greed-greed? Or profits-profits-profits? Or "Screw the other guy before he screws you!" Remember, business does not happen in a vacuum. It is a social enterprise. Your customers, clients, coworkers, and contacts are not just abstract entities on a spreadsheet; they are human beings.

How successful you are depends in part on how successfully you relate with other people, and how you make them feel: happy? Sad? Indifferent? Angry? Like they're being cheated or talked down to? Respect others, and they will respect you. Sound like something you were told in elementary school? Exactly. It is one of those elemental facts about human beings. Reflect on it, absorb it, and recognize its truth.

So, getting along with others is important. But in order for you to get along with others, you must first get along with yourself. It's sort of like a twist on the Golden Rule: Become the kind of person you'd like to get to know. Become the kind of person whom, if you met him or her out in the world somewhere, would intrigue you, would inspire trust and confidence. The kind of person you would want to befriend and have on your side.

An old friend of mine who was a Vietnam Veteran had a formula for assessing people's character. He asked himself, "Is this the kind of person I'd want with me in a foxhole?" He was in no way suggesting that he'd want the most macho, most violent, most foolhardy, or even bravest. What he meant was that the most important traits were smarts, trustworthiness, and the ability to keep a cool head and good attitude while under pressure. Most essential: be someone who radiates positivity.

Negativity is a dark and hateful cloud. There is so much of it in this world, and it's way more contagious than avian flu. How wonderful a world this would be if only positivity and happiness were even half as catching as negativity and discontent! Have you ever noticed how one unreasonably angry or pessimistic person can destroy the good vibes of an entire room of people, and sour the moods of the most naturally cheerful? Why doesn't a radiant smile or an encouraging word have the same power to disperse brooding and depression?

Perhaps it's just the way of human beings to respond more easily to what is unhealthy or unhelpful. Try to make your positivity shine like a lantern—let good vibes light up the room, and keep the interfering demon of negativity at bay. You will see how eagerly people respond to the magnetic aura of positive thinking. When people are feeling positive and optimistic, they do their best and most creative thinking.

Remember too that negativity and positivity are their own feedback loops. When you put negativity out into the world, that's what you get back. The same goes for positivity. Negative people often think the world is out to get them. They think most people are rude and don't give them the respect they deserve. It's probably the case that a person like this hasn't taken the time to ask themselves, "Am I just getting back what I put in?" Sure, people can be rude.

But nine times out of ten I find that a friendly approach to people gets a friendly response. What you sow, you shall reap.

When negative vibes attach to us, we take them everywhere: to the gym, school, church, home, and work. They're like dust on our shoes or on our shoulder, and we track them everywhere. We spread negativity to our friends, family and co-workers. We each have an aura or energy, and emit whatever is in our hearts and minds, even if on a subtle or subliminal level. That energy flows freely, infecting the weak and strong both, corroding group morale. Stronger spirits will hold out longer, but eventually the eroding effects of negativity take their toll. I've always believed that some people get a perverse thrill out of spreading discontent. But once you start spreading positivity, and seeing how that confidence infects other people, you will no longer want to be a source of bad feelings.

The ease of spreading negativity seems especially true of the workplace. When morale is high, companies are like a well-oiled machine, with everybody performing at their utmost level. When morale is low, the gears grind to a halt. What may have been a sturdy edifice is now a house of cards, and no doubt you can hear it creaking ominously above your head. Think of the door to your workplace as having a guard station. But instead of checking in your weapons or other contraband, the guards insist you relinquish your pessimism, naysaying, and bad attitude.

Being fired is no fun. But I promise you, having to fire somebody is no picnic either. It's hard to tell somebody they've failed to meet whatever expectations you've had of them. I have had the extreme displeasure of having to fire employees due to personal issues with drugs, disrespect, a threatening demeanor, or simply an inability to get along with their coworkers.

I don't think I've ever made a bad hiring decision. In fact, everybody I've had to let go was great in the beginning. But somewhere along the way they tripped over one of life's stumbling blocks and couldn't regain their footing. Their bad attitude was wearing other people down. As the founder of a company, I felt that my business was a reflection on me. Being a good person and making a good living are not mutually exclusive. I want any company, whether it's one I've founded or one I'm working for, to reflect my values. I want it to be a positive influence on the world.

Dragging your personal life into work is one of those major business Don'ts that we all know in principle, but often have a hard time practicing. One can see today that many visionary CEO's are trying to sync people's personal and professional lives as harmoniously as possible. They turn workplaces into social environments, so that coworkers feel like family and friends. There are company cafeterias, bars, daycares, schools, restaurants and exercise facilities.

This is wonderful, and I commend the effort. But for the most part companies are still just places of business, and not our communities—this will probably always be the case, as much as we as a society try to make life and work overlap and more closely correspond to one another. We may be very close with our co-workers, to the point where they feel like friends and even family. Still, it is important not to forget that the relationship is first and foremost a professional one.

As a man who has seen what kinds of things adversely affect a company from every angle—entry-level employee, supervisor, founder; top, bottom, and middle—this principle can never be stressed enough. We all have troubles in our personal lives, stresses that are difficult to shrug off when we set out for work. But putting on your work clothes should be like a superhero putting on his costume. You are becoming your alter ego; your costume and cape are impervious to bullets and flames; you must put on a brave face to go fight villainy.

Even Superman had a lot of personal problems. In a way, he was a foster child who never got to know his parents. He was in love with a woman whom he had to lie to constantly. He was sometimes burdened by his role as a savior to mankind. But you didn't see him carrying this heavy baggage along with him when it was time to go duke it out with Lex Luther. Take care of business first, and save the rest for later.

This is not to say that our personal lives are less important than our professional lives. Most of us, if forced to choose between a dearly loved one and, say, a significant raise, would most certainly opt for the loved one. But there is a feedback loop between professional and personal. When you bring those negative aspects of your personal life into work, you darken all your professional dealings, which then are brought back into your personal life, so that both become corrupted, and both start to fall apart.

Strong personal relationships need firm footing, and economic security is a major part of that solid ground. It may even be the most important. One of things people who love one another most often argue about is money. Money issues are cited as the primary cause for divorce in the vast majority of failed marriages. Economic security brings emotional security. Taking care of business will better allow you to focus on personal issues.

Before you take your economic security for granted, take stock of where you are. First of all, you are very lucky to even have a job. Being employed is nothing to take lightly. No, your boss can't read your mind, but do you think he or she won't notice if you're dragging your life's sewage into the workplace on the soles of your shoes? Trust me, it will stink up the place, and if you do it too often nobody will be able to ignore the stench.

Imagine yourself sitting at your desk, personal problems consuming all your energy and attention. Let's get hypothetical, and pretend your life reads like the lyrics to the saddest country song ever written. Your son is in prison and your daughter in rehab. Your spouse wants a divorce and says they never wanted to get married in the first place. You have $100 in your bank account, your credit cards are maxed, your home is in foreclosure, and the bank wants to repossess your car. Your dog had surgery and the vet is sending your bill to collections. Your mother is sick and your dad is leaving her for another woman. Your brother just got a DUI and your sister just joined a cult and gave them all of her money. To top it off, all this was sprung on you the week before Thanksgiving, and now you have no idea who's going to cook the turkey. And frankly, you're starting to feel like your turkey is already cooked.

So your head is swirling, the world is crashing in around you, and you're wondering how you can possibly put a smile on your face. You just want to crawl in a hole, disappear, drown in your tears and never return. Yet through it all, you have your daily commitment of going to work. You have to earn a living. But with your mind tangled up with so many distractions, problems pulling your thoughts in every direction, your head is full of noise and you can't focus.

Ask yourself, what can you do about any of these troubles right now? Most likely, absolutely nothing! Even supposing you can, how are you going to justify spending time on the phone trying to put fires out on your boss's dime, or texting when nobody's looking? Will losing your job or being put on probation help solve your problems? I should think not.

Abraham Maslow was a psychologist who put together a pyramid, each level representing a human need that, when met, allowed the individual to concentrate on fulfilling his or her next level of needs. His idea was that a person had to settle one aspect of their life before being able to concentrate on another. At the bottom are basic things like food, water and shelter. Just above that are employment and property. Still further up the pyramid are human relationships. Maslow demonstrated that for you to have the good life, you needed to have your bases covered and your basics taken care of. So don't take employment for granted! It's the base upon which your mighty pyramid is built!

Something else to consider. It is a truth proven time and time again all throughout history. Sometimes the brain, the unconscious brain, does its best thinking when the conscious mind is occupied elsewhere. Often a brilliant solution will come into your head when you don't even know your brain is dwelling upon a problem and working out a solution. Many great ideas were worked out while a person was occupied with other things, or even sleeping. Focus your energy elsewhere, while being assured that at the back of your mind the problems are still being considered by some part of yourself. Then, on your own free time, there is a good chance you will have a clearer head and will be better able to tackle whatever challenges are burdening your spirit. Maybe your mind has even already solved the problem! Set upon your priorities, the tasks at hand, and let what needs working out work itself out naturally, in its own due course.

What Drives You?

Before we discuss attaining financial success, we first have to take an honest look at our values. For many people, success doesn't have a financial component to it at all. There are many business speakers who say you shouldn't hang around with poor people. They say that in order to become rich, you must associate with the rich. They will tell you that in order for you to become rich, you must be involved with the rich, act like the rich, smell like the rich, drive a car like the rich, eat like the rich and dress like the rich.

The element of truth in this is that it's helpful to spend time with people who are involved in economic endeavors; people for whom making money is not a complete mystery. You may be put in touch with people who can help you with investments and business deals, and you may benefit from an insider's perspective.

But really—do we want to be the kind of people who avoid other human beings simply because they won't add numerical value to our bottom line? I am here to tell you that some of the richest people I know are the poorest financially. They are rich in spirit. The accumulation of money is not their goal, but rather the accumulation of meaningful life experiences and time for the things they love.

Remember, becoming financially well-off is just one of many possible goals. Life is not all about the dollar; it's about time well spent. If making money is what gets you revved, the more power to you. Business is truly exciting, and playing the game is invigorating. So yes, making money can certainly be part of the good life. But before you go believing it's the only important thing, take a moment to reflect honestly on your priorities.

A truly successful person is one whose life is significant. I sometimes ask myself, if I was to die tomorrow, what mark did I leave upon this Earth? I want people's memories of me to be good ones. I want to think I was a force for positive change. A small kindness perpetrated today can echo for generations to come. That said, making money can be an opportunity for you to do good; and making lots of money can be an opportunity for you to do lots of good.

Look at Bill Gates; he has done more good for this world than perhaps any single human being who has ever lived. And with the charitable funds he has set up, his legacy of good deeds will continue long after he is gone. But without pure capitalistic ambitions, without the drive to turn his fledgling company Microsoft into the global behemoth it is today, the millions of people who have benefited from his generosity would have been left with a Bill Gates-sized hole in their lives.

I like that most companies participate in philanthropic projects that help their community. The biggest corporations have donated millions to help those suffering from major catastrophes, and fund wonderful public service projects. I am not cynical enough to think these efforts are mere public relations ploys. Doing good instead of evil is a major morale booster, and people will work harder when they feel the organization they're employed by is a force for good in the world.

To find success, we have to know what motivates us. Ask yourself if you are doing what you really want to be doing. You will spend the majority of your life working. You should love your job. If you don't, find one you do. If you love it, you will excel at it. Don't be one of those poor souls who stuck with a job their entire lives just because it meant security. Life is not secure. You could be walking down the sidewalk tomorrow and a piano might fall on your head. You might be crossing the street and be hit by a runaway bus.

So before that piano or bus gets you, ask yourself if you are working a job that gives you the rewards you really care about? Maybe you'd be willing to take a job for less pay at a non-profit? Perhaps there is something besides money that gets you up and out of bed in the morning. We must first determine our passion and discover what really moves us if we are going to be victorious in any endeavor. If after soul-searching you do find that financial success is your motivator, then it's time to go about seeking your fortune.

If you don't feel like you are a success yet, or are wondering how you might raise your standard of living, there are some comforting thoughts. First, it does the insecure spirit well to remember: a successful person wasn't always so. When we're on the bottom of the heap looking up at those flashy folks who seem on top of the world, it can be mighty tempting to think those people were always there, eating with silver spoons and having pie-in-the-sky for dessert.

I tell you, I have known many successful people who built their empires from the bottom up, with no more capital investment than their dreams, determination, and faith. Most people were not born at the top—they were not handed their success. But then, you might tell yourself, perhaps these successful folk have a certain drive or personality trait that I don't share and could never hope to acquire. I'm telling you again: not true!

Yes, it does indeed take certain traits to succeed, but these are traits that are available to everybody, habits of mind and body that can be adopted, nurtured, and developed. We are all just humans being after all. In this sense we all have a clean slate; we all share the same abilities and potential. I have been poor, believe me—lower than the dirt on your Reebok sneakers. I know how it feels to be on the outside looking in, wondering, "How did they do it?" and, "Could it ever be me?" Well I don't necessarily know how *they* did it, but I know how I did it. And could it ever be you? Of course it can! Don't ever doubt that fact. Knowing that you could be where your heroes or mentors are is the first brick to lay in your edifice of personal achievement.

Okay sure, I'll give you this: some people were indeed born rich. You already know this. We all know it! Some people were born with all the financial security in the world. They always had disposable income at the ready. They had a well-woven safety net hung beneath them, so that any risks or endeavors that failed led to nothing more dire than a soft landing several feet above the hard reality of ground. Heck, they probably drove nicer cars to high school than the ones your parents owned. But it doesn't matter how much we have been given, what matters is what we do with what has been given.

As you've heard said before, no risk means no reward. You have to go out on a limb to achieve your dreams. It's not about who does or doesn't have more resources, or a better safety net. Making sacrifices and taking risks is always a component to turning dreams into reality. Some people's risks are riskier, yes, but if you are going to be successful, you have to be willing to put all your chips on the table. Big risk equals big returns.

I would also warn you to be cautious about thinking easy privilege is its own reward, or any reward at all. I have met children of wealthy parents. It truly can be a curse. First off, there may be greater expectations placed on the child, expectations that are either unnatural to his or her character, or simply too heavy a burden to bear. They also often lack the hunger that makes the pursuit of success an adventure. We have all seen many a trust-fund funded child wander off into a life of listlessness, substance abuse, and wasted potential. They are often ungrounded, and unable to keep both feet planted firmly on terra firma. They may become jackals, but have a harder time becoming wolves.

Don't you know that hard times create a riveted soul? A hardy spirit? There is an exhilarating vigor and life-affirming animalism that comes from having to give chase. Feel your limbs flex, and your spirit give flight! You are an untamed soul, and a little hardship will keep you from getting flabby, soft, and arrogant. You will take nothing for granted. And if you don't think that alone is a great gift, then you and I are not cut from the same cloth.

You must also get beyond the mindset that accuses successful people of not having earned their wealth or accolades. A resentful attitude is unhealthy, and your drive to succeed should come from within your own beating heart, not be the heated spur of external envies. Everybody has seen their share of let-downs, believe me. And if they're successful today, I guarantee they still experience professional failures. Big sales and important deals will slip through their fingers like sand.

The best baseball player swings and misses. The best basketball player tosses a brick and misses the winning shot. The best quarterback throws an interception when the pressure is on and every play counts. Likewise, even the most motivated and promising salesperson will lose a deal here and there. It just happens. Business is like life, it has ups and downs, wins and losses, sadness and happiness. It is never predictable, and one can always expect the unexpected. In business as in life, what you do when the going gets tough makes all the difference.

Though it's perhaps a little trite to divide the world up into two kinds of people, it can be a useful exercise. Generally, there are reactionary types and proactive types. After considering your past, in what category do you place yourself? This is one of the most important pieces to the puzzle that is your personal and professional success. Many people don't make a move until they're forced to respond to life's circumstances.

They procrastinate, put off important decisions, and fail to act at the most opportune time. Often when we're forced to react, we fail to take time to consider a strategy or thoughtful plan. We're caught on our back heels, and our imbalance leads to an imperfect response. How much better to meet a challenge with one foot forward, steadied at our center of balance, ready to spring forth and wrestle with our opponent.

As Marine Corps officers are taught: even an imperfectly executed action is more productive than no action, or a response to somebody else's moves. When we make proactive moves, we're filled with a life-affirming confidence and a sense of control over our destiny. Sure, you will have to improvise. Your action will inspire reaction, and you will have to act again in response to new developments. But as long as you are on the offensive, you will find yourself in a better position to take advantage of opportunity. As the German writer Goethe said, "Whatever you do, or dream you can, begin it. Boldness has power and magic in it." Taking the first step and putting yourself out there will bring many immediate rewards. Take a leap of faith, and new opportunities will come to you in spades. Trust me on this.

I honestly believe that the bad habit of reactivity is the primary reason people get hooked on drugs and alcohol, or live lives full of anger and sadness. Outward events become like strong winds, blowing hard against us and tossing us about willy-nilly. Soon we feel like we have no control over the world around us. This feeling of being blown about as a plaything of fate is depressing, and bogs us down in self-pity and hopelessness. Instead of believing we might be able to take control of fate and set out on a rewarding path toward ultimate victory, we content ourselves with nurturing and cultivating our own self-doubts. We spiral into despair, and seek oblivion in chemical substances or their only slightly less damaging counterparts: sloth, procrastination, and cynicism.

Contrary to a popular adage, opportunity does not come knocking. You have to go knocking on its door. Whatever thrill a person gets from drugs and alcohol is tripled or quadrupled by going out and actively engaging life. Be a participant, not a spectator. You will find yourself suddenly involved in existence, and this feeling is the strongest high you can get.

Character, Character, Character

Remember, character is everything. Most of us were born with the ability to know right from wrong. Unless we're complete sociopaths, we possess a moral compass. It is the tendency of older men and women to look at the modern world and think things have gotten far worse. That people are less moral, and don't hold themselves to as high an ethical standard as they have in times past. Whether this is true or not, it does seem that somewhere along the way the line dividing right from wrong was moved.

We see that the current economic crisis was brought about in large part because people were behaving in immoral ways, justifying shady actions and in the end bringing down some of the most prestigious names in the corporate world. The actions of a few greedy individuals shook confidence in financial institutions across the globe. Even if people really are no worse than in previous eras, the scope of their wicked ways is much broader.

It's truly tragic when a life spent making all the right moves gets derailed by something idiotic. The headlines are unbelievable. If we're the type of person who pays attention, we can hear of a teacher sleeping with a student in the morning, a manager pointing a gun in an employee's face by lunch, and before getting home for dinner, an employee embezzling money from the very company that gave them their first big chance. Every day on TV, in magazines and the internet, we hear about some wildly off-color behavior from a person who seemed to have everything going for them. These people literally wasted their life by losing control.

Think of how profound this is: somebody literally wasted their precious life. Remember the female astronaut who drove across the country in a diaper in order to avenge herself on her lover? She must have worked so hard to get where she was! And she had her dream job! Obviously love makes us do crazy things, but get a grip!

Don't ever throw your career away by caving in to a temporary emotion.

I must confess, I have a very difficult time putting myself inside the mind of someone who was willing to throw it all away on an irrational whim or overwhelming passion. I've always been the type of person who, once my goal is set and identified, I am locked and loaded. I keep my "eyes on the prize." There are some who might say about the above case concerning the astronaut, that she was derailed by love. That love makes us do crazy things we wouldn't even consider if such a strong emotion wasn't guiding us and overpowering our reason.

I understand that love makes us lose our minds sometimes. But I have a slightly different take on the matter. I think those who excuse her behavior in this way are putting the effect before the cause. I say that if her instincts hadn't been faulty to begin with, she wouldn't have been derailed in the first place. I say that her instincts were already tottering if she allowed herself to be so derailed. It just goes to show you that it is doubly important that you have firm footing from the start, and this firm footing comes from developing the personal strength that keeps you focused on what really matters.

Be Here Now!

This is one HUGE problem with our society! Most people aren't living in the present moment, the here and now. You share the planet with billions of people, but how many are truly in their life's moment right this second? We cannot change the past, and each second carries us into the future. Meanwhile, there is the present to be attended to. People are far too focused on the past, or living so far in their future they don't notice what's going on around them. It's like their minds are spread thin across the fourth dimension. As an old Irish proverb says, "Don't waste too many of your todays on yesterday."

Here is a little secret: the future is right now. Yesterday you thought about today, which in my mind means you were living in it. Tomorrow you will think about today. Eventually, the future will leave you behind. You will wake up one day and realize that you never even lived in the present. Don't spend your time riding on a slow train back to the past; buy a ticket for a high-speed train to a future destination.

Every morning you wake up is like having a second chance, or an opportunity to change course in life. You open your eyes, and there is a fresh white canvas waiting to be painted on. Even if we don't plan on making major changes on a given day, it helps to have an attitude of gratitude and just be thankful we woke up. There are thousands of people who didn't, and I have no doubt all of them would trade places with us if they could. Don't let the mundane day-in, day-out suppress your sense of awe. It is not sophomoric to take a moment to reflect on how amazing the simple fact of your existence is.

You are real, you are a person. The sky and the stars and the planets are real. Plants and animals and all the amazing things around us are miracles, as are the fact that we are privileged enough to be conscious of it. As philosophers have asked for centuries, "Why something instead of nothing?" Life is a sublime and wonderful mystery, and taking a moment now and again to recognize it as such can help ground us. So times are hard: the very fact that we exist to experience the struggle is enough to amaze us and shake us out of our complacency.

I have found that merely being grateful for the air I breathe helps me put life in perspective. It inspires me to get the most out of every day. As far as I know, I have one life to live. I intend to live it. Time and time again, I have seen people who have died long before they're actually dead and in the grave. They are living miserable lives because they hold onto something—some pain, some insecurity, some fear or some hatred—that will not allow them to live their life to the fullest. A wise man once said that you must die before you can really live. What I take this to mean is that you must cease to be so concerned with your own life that you forget what it means to have life! It means you've been given the chance to do something amazing.

Whenever I see somebody just going through the motions of life, I have the urge to check their pulse. Do they realize an exciting and invigorating life could be theirs if they just opened their eyes to life? We live in a country blessed with bountiful freedoms. We can come and go as we please. If we're down in the dumps in one place, we can move. If our career or lifestyle is bogging us down, we can head overseas for an invigorating intercultural adventure. Just volunteering to help the poor can make us more appreciative of what we have been given.

Sometimes you see wisdom in the strangest places. I once read the following on a button: "If you don't like your lot in life, change your life a lot." Maybe your environment isn't providing the opportunities you seek. Well, a bus ticket is pretty cheap. Look at a map for a better locale, and if you decide it's right for you, hit the road. New adventures are always just around the corner.

Here are a few things to consider when evaluating your current way of thinking. Ask yourself these questions:

Am I self-sufficient? Do I thrive or simply survive? Does unbalance control me or do I control my balance? Does time control me or do I control my time? Does money control me or do I control my money? Does food control me or do I control my food? Does anger control me or do I control my anger? Does passion control me or do I control my passion? Do I try to find the humor in the things, or do I take things too seriously? Do I live life to the fullest or do I live life with no fullness?

Don't be the person laying on their deathbed regretting not having done what they always wanted to. Imagine your future self, looking back on what you did with your days and nights. Ask if this person had the guts to throw caution to the wind and just go for it. It's a morbid thought, but one any mature adult must accept: the cemetery isn't going anywhere; it will always be waiting for you. And you don't have to be deceased to be a ghost.

Every day of our life spent wallowing in a situation we'd prefer not to be is like being a ghoul or a specter, haunting our own home, workplace, and the city we live in. A wasted day is a day living as a shadow of our true selves. Taking the safe and boring way guarantees you will have major regrets one day. How much better to live the exciting life! A life full of curiosity and opportunity! Feel the blood rushing through your veins and the air filling your lungs. You are alive! You are a beast!

Chances are that if you procrastinate in one aspect of your life, such as business, you will procrastinate in others, such as your personal life. You must live your life with urgency in order to accomplish your dreams. So: Procrastinate or Proactivate? The way you answer this question determines your destiny. It's that simple. You have two choices in life, TO DO or TO NOT DO. Not choosing is also a choice. At every juncture in our life there is a fork in the road, and at least two paths. Both ways are riddled with uncertainties and unknowns. But as you stand there wondering what to do, you're losing momentum. Choose, and let the path not taken recede into the distance.

The great thing about your life is that you alone decide your outcome through your actions. When you're debating between

doing and not doing, it will only be action
that finally decides. Choices don't have to
be major, life-altering affairs. Start out
small—baby steps! All the tiny moments—
the seconds, minutes, and hours—added
together determine the quality of your
future. Every moment provides you with an
opportunity to work toward a future that will
profit you mentally, spiritually, and
financially. Start with some small matter,
and soon you will feel more comfortable
taking the grandest leaps of faith.

Excuses: Fear and Faith

Never put off until tomorrow what you can do today. Right. Few people will argue that being proactive is a bad thing. But if it's so clearly a good, then what holds so many of us back from taking decisive action? I find it hard to believe it's fear of success, as I often hear people say. The common wisdom tells us that some people fear success because they are afraid they will not be able to live up to their achievements, and that success will bring new challenges and responsibilities they may not be able to handle. They feel success might expose their flaws, and that whatever success they achieved could have been mere luck or happenstance.

These are of course valid concerns, but I believe "fear of success" is just a conceptual twist that masks what the real matter is: fear of failure. Fearing the unanticipated consequences of success is just another way of saying you fear your success will lead to future failures. Once we have banished the fear of failure, we banish its supposed opposite, the fear of success.

Fear of failure makes you sweep your ideas, whether brilliant or outlandish, under the rug. It makes you hide your desire to dream big, as if it were some kind of deformity or shameful scar. Fear makes us dread both the possible and the impossible, the mundane and realistic no less than the fantastic and seemingly unattainable. As Brendan Francis said, "Many of our fears are tissue-paper thin, and a single courageous step would carry us clear through them."

Overcoming limiting thoughts can be a habit. Every time you catch a thought designed to limit your ambitions or desires running through your mind, consciously send up a red flag. Put it up as a warning to step cautiously when your mind goes to this place in the future. Over time, you will catch yourself returning to this place, and you can steer clear. Negativity is a habit of mind. When you warn yourself away from negative thoughts, you won't let those ruts run deep. Most importantly, remember: you never fail until you stop trying. So try, try, try, and try again.

Failure is a judgment that is social in nature. If we lived in a vacuum and had no one else to compare ourselves with, or somebody whose expectations we felt we had to meet, failure would not even exist as a concept. We can only be failures in the eyes of other human beings. We all want others to have a positive image of us. We don't want people to see us fall flat on our face and smirk at our misfortune. But it comes down to this: you have to learn to say, "Screw what others think of me!"

Life is an adventure. On any adventure, failure is a possibility. People who live adventurous lives understand this. The first person to climb Mt. Everest or journey to the center of the North Pole knew they might not make it. But they gave it their best, didn't they? If somebody mocks you for failing, take heart in the fact that they must not be familiar with the spirit of adventure.

We have to get beyond the kind of thinking that assumes our own failures as the end of the world. Put your life in perspective. You share the planet with over six billion people. Over eighty billion people have lived on this Earth. Earth is a tiny planet in an immense solar system, which is itself just a teensy-tiny speck of dust in an enormous galaxy. The Milky Way galaxy is itself only one of billions.

Compared to the cosmic ballet occurring on a stage that is light-years wide, what is the meaning of your failures? They are nothing; they are blips. All this is not to diminish the importance of your life. What I'm saying is that in the end, anything we do is only the tiniest part of the whole, so why should we worry about failure? So you fail. The Earth still turns, the planets make their orbits, and the sun doesn't fall from the sky. Being insignificant—at least in the grand scheme of things—buys us limitless freedom to experiment.

Anyone who ridicules or pokes fun at a person who is trying is the real "loser." Rest assured, those who criticize others are only expressing their own insecurities. We are all just human beings, caught up in the mystery of life. The person looking down on you is just as entangled in it, whether he is a captain of industry or your next-door neighbor. He was born a helpless baby, and will die a helpless old man. Charles Dickens began his classic tale, *A Christmas Carol*, saying that Christmas was "the only time when men open their shut-up hearts and think of all people as fellow travelers to the grave and not some other race of creatures bound on other journeys."

Well, why can't every day be Christmas, in this sense? Why can't we see all human beings as fellow travelers on the journey of life? It can be a spur to compassion just as it can be a shield from judgment. From dust we come, and to dust we shall return—the prince and pauper, professor and ignoramus alike. People's opinions simply do not matter. This idea is a powerful tool in letting judgments roll off our back.

Visualize results; it will help you bolster conviction and faith in your goal. Imagine the you who has already achieved your goals—how did he get there? What steps did he have to take? What landmines did he have to sidestep, snake-pits did he have to leap over, contacts did he have to make, opportunities did he have to explore? Take a look at your bank statement. How does it make you feel? Do you wish the numbers were bigger, and that there were more commas? See your future self tearing open your statement and sighing with happiness, comfort, and security. What investments did you have to make? What changes did you have to make in the way you thought about money? Where did you have to put your financial resources to gain returns? What hard work did you have to do in order to see those numbers appear? What seminars did you have to attend, or books did you have to read, in order to break loose from the shackles that kept you from just going for it? We know these kinds of results are attainable because we see people everyday who have attained them. There is no reason you cannot be one of them.

Say to yourself right now: "I AM LIMITLESS! NOTHING CAN HOLD ME BACK! I HAVE ENDLESS POTENTIAL

AND ENDLESS ENERGY! I CAN DO
ANYTHING I PUT MY MIND TO!"

Don't ever let excuses steal victory out of
your hands. Let an excuse be slippery and
slimy like an eel: hard to grasp and even
harder to keep hold of. If you find an excuse
leaping into your hand and trying to make
itself comfortable there, grab it by the throat
and throttle the life out of it. Whatever you
do, don't coddle it like a babe. It is a vile
thing, and should be dropped. Instead of
being attached to your problems, why not
strive to nurture an attachment to your
dreams? A human being only has so much
energy; indeed, a rather limited amount.
Where we invest our mental and emotional
resources leads directly to returns on that
investment. If you put money in bad stocks,
you can expect bad dividends.

Excuses exhaust us, because as they build
up we must become apologists for them,
justifying their presence. This takes up
energy we could be applying to more
constructive ends. Excuses are little
gremlins, hiding in every nook and cranny.
We must bring them into the light so we can

have good, clear look at them, and see how ugly they really are. Have you used any of these commonplace excuses at some point in your life?

"I'm afraid. It's too hard and too risky. I'll probably fail if I try, because I'm not smart enough and nothing good ever happens to me. Besides, I've already tried and wasn't strong enough. I don't have the time or the talent and will probably just botch it up. I always lose, and I worry what people will think of me if I fail. I've tried it a million times and it just won't work."

With a little courage, you can always accomplish something unprecedented. In fact, the more unprecedented your goal, the more courage you will need! And you may not think living uncomfortably takes courage, but it truly does. Most people strive to attain a certain level of convenience and ease. They think there will come a time when they can just kick their feet up and not have to lift another finger in effort. Comfort is frequently a goal in itself. But how many people have asked themselves whether or not comfort is really a goal worth striving for? Physical comfort does have its uses—it gives you a nice little foundation for you to get mentally uncomfortable.

Life can and will be overwhelming at times. I don't know a single soul who has lived a productive and admirable life and said that it was easy. Life is full of surprises, and not all of them will be pleasant. Discomfort is always crouching, ready to pounce into your life and upset your pleasant little repose. But discomfort only becomes an enemy when we think of it as such. Think of discomfort as an ally. Discomfort forces you to act, make decisions, and strategize. Welcome it into your life as a friend who taps you on the shoulder and says, "Buddy, you are way too full of life to live the life of leisure." A little stress and pressure force us to be creative and make moves.

Becoming a champion starts in the mind, with your own thoughts. A champion's mentality begins with the belief that he or she can be better than the best, by being faster, smarter and stronger. They are determined, and already know they have the power within them to achieve their goal. They believe it, speak it, practice it, and live it. Of course they may lose the race, or not set the world record. But they don't let these failures become permanent evaluations of themselves. Next time, they think, I'll definitely do it next time.

We are all born with the potential to be a champion, but this potential is destroyed when we allow others to destroy our belief in ourselves. Remember to populate your mind with cheerleaders. Even when cheerleaders cheer for a team that loses, you see them on the sidelines at the next game, acting as if last week's defeat never happened. Don't be afraid to give yourself a good "Rah! Rah!", even if last week you didn't pull out a victory.

Something worth keeping in mind is that you can save another person's life after you have saved your own. If you don't think doing your best for yourself is its own reward, you will find that doing your best so that you can help others do theirs is just as moving and motivating, if not more so. Helping another person see value in life is a life-changing experience, but it's best achieved when you see value in your own.

Convince another person they can give a great gift to the world, then watch them do it. You will be elated beyond your wildest dreams. By offering your talents and wisdom to the world, you can literally change the course of this crazy planet. You never know who you will inspire, and what you might inspire them to do. Pay it forward, as they say, and you never have to doubt that you have made a difference.

So never give up. Find the faith within to fuel your spirit. Believe in your vision. Believe in yourself and believe that you have a lot to offer. Use your life to put your stamp on the world. You are unique. Only you can offer the world that one thing it really needs. Thomas Edison tried over 10,000 times to invent the light bulb. Through perseverance and hard work, he did it. You may not be here to invent the light bulb, but trust me when I tell you that you have your own gift to offer this world. Believe it!

Who Do You Surround Yourself With?

You become the product of your environment. A major component of success is the company you keep. We've already discussed how unrealistic and inhuman it is to avoid people who you feel won't bring you closer to your financial goals. However, it's a good idea to hang out with people who laugh a lot and are uplifting. Realize that there will come a time when you may have to let go of certain friends.

Peers begin to influence us more than family at a very early age. As a child, it can be difficult to reflect on how people affect your life. Hopefully by the time you are an adult, you will have a better sense of who is good for you and who isn't. Some friends are good for certain seasons of your life, but if the friendship is destructive to yourself and your goals, you must move on. There is a reason in your great destiny that someone will walk in your life and then walk out.

I've had good and bad friends. My good friends had my back—they wanted what was best for me. They wanted to see me succeed and realize my dreams. Some friends are weary of your successes—they feel it detracts from them, or worry they'll be seen in a less than flattering light if they aren't as motivated as you. That's ridiculous! Friends are important, and should want to share in your glories and console you when you make missteps. Friends should help you become a better person. Don't be afraid to let the wrong friends go, so you can make room in your life for the right friends.

I do my best to ignore negative people who throw off a toxic vibe. I don't want to surround myself with doubters and "doom-and-gloomers." I know that some of you can change your life right now by changing your friends. Find people who dare to dream of changing the world and making it a better place. Avoid those who belittle your dreams, or think it's impossible to do anything great. I once heard a saying: "Do you want to fly with the eagles or fly with the chickens?" The eagle is the highest-soaring bird; a chicken can only go a few feet off the ground. As for myself, I know I want to be flying with eagles, and going where they go. The view is much better.

Wherever you happen to be in life, there is somebody out there who has already walked the same road. Sure, nobody has walked in your shoes specifically, but there are all kinds of people who have walked in similar ones: the same size, shape, and brand. Our life experiences are unique in the particulars—but when it comes to the broad strokes, we are not alone. If you want to understand how life operates, ask someone older than you. Chances are they have been where you are, or know how to avoid the pitfalls you're at risk of falling into. The older they are, the wiser they should be.

Seeking counsel from those with a wide range of experience needn't mean we take their word as our step-by-step guide to life. After all, we must make our own mistakes in order to learn from them. But whenever you come across somebody who has something to offer, don't neglect to take advantage of the opportunity to learn something new.

I have spoken to many successful salespeople. Some who make several hundred thousand dollars a year, and some who make millions; even a few that regularly make a couple hundred million a year. Their nuggets of wisdom are invaluable. Even if their experience is not directly relatable to yours, just to hear their anecdotes is amazing. You get an inside glimpse of the real ins and outs of the business world, and for somebody like me who is naturally curious, you couldn't ask for a better way to spend a few hours.

In the past I have paid a lot of money to spend some time with these successful people so I could get to know their strategies, pick their brains, and find out how their mind works. Never be afraid to ask a successful person questions. They might be busy, but if they have the time they're usually more than happy to let you in on a few of their secrets.

Once I flew to another state for a night to speak with a relative's friend who had just closed a 400 million dollar commercial real estate deal and pocketed 250 million. At the time it was mindboggling to me: just how was he able to pull off such an amazing feat? So I contacted him, and based on the referral from my relative, he told me he was open to meeting me and granting me an interview. I arrived in the early evening at his luxurious 14,000 square foot home. It was gorgeous. His place reminded me of the Hearst Castle. I was able to hang out with him for a few hours and he was gracious enough to put up with me. Here are some of the questions I asked him and the answers he gave.

What is your favorite book? *Think and Grow Rich.*

How have you overcome your obstacles and failures? *You just find a way. Keep going forward. Become more creative and don't worry about being ridiculed for trying something new.*

What would you say has been your greatest sacrifice? *Time with friends and family.*

Does intuition or logic direct you in making choices? *Intuition*

What time to you get up? *5 am.*

What time do you go to bed? *10 pm.*

Would you say that you reinvent yourself? *Yes I reinvent myself every now and then.*

Do you like to go on vacation? *Yes, vacations are a must especially when you are under pressure. It takes your mind off things for a while so you can refocus and be in the present moment.*

Are you always a positive person? *Not always. I am a realist. I am brutally honest.*

Do you typically take risky opportunities and would you describe yourself as a risk taker? *No. I don't like to take risks. I try to keep it minimized and focus on the outcome.*

How do you sustain the energy that drives you without getting burnt out? *I like to change things up and rest, take a break from the project to refocus. The wins pick you up but the losses are demoralizing.*

What is the #1 business rule you live by? *"Whatever the mind of man can conceive and believe, it can achieve." By Napolean Hill*

How do you keep getting better? *Self-improvement books and seminars.*

How would you describe your steps to success? *Self-discipline makes you successful. Be fair in all of your business dealings.*

Do you ever find yourself thinking about fear, doubt, rejections, or embarrassment? *No*

Are you fearful of living in poverty or not making enough? *No, I have skills. I earned it, I will earn it again.*

Have you always pictured yourself wealthy and having this huge luxurious home? *YES!*

What would you say is your life purpose? *To help other people become millionaires.*

What would you say has been your greatest achievement? *My box of thank you cards from others. Wealth magnifies the good and the bad in people. It is nice to know that I have magnified the good.*

I.R.O.C.K.

Dwelling on the past is like being tied down by an anchor or ball and chain. It holds us frozen in one place, even as time rushes on. You must be able to let things go. This isn't always easy, I understand. I will be the first to admit that the pain of my past has infected me and held me back. I've been lost, not knowing what direction to take in life. There have been times when all I could think was, "Why me?" But when you hit rock bottom, the only way to go is up.

Everyone suffers, but what we do with that suffering makes all the difference. Pain can be a tool that helps us shape our future. When you change the way you think about your pain, your life changes in dramatic ways. I realized as a young man that I didn't have to feel guilty and blame myself for the pain my mother and father caused me. I had to take responsibility for my own life and not let bad memories control my attitude. I realized that I wanted to be a victor in life and no longer a victim. I wanted to ROCK!

There is a simple formula that I use to bring more meaning into my life. It is a program I teach when I do seminars. It is called I-R.O.C.K. It is an acronym for how I live my life, as well as how I inspire others to live theirs.

I is for Integrity
R is for Responsibility
O is for Opportunity
C is for Choice
K is for Knowledge

Integrity is the most important quality. It is measured by how well we live up to our core principles and values. Often we fail to meet our own standards and expectations, but if we gave it our best shot, our integrity remains intact. The part of you that holds yourself accountable to a higher standard is the person who assesses your integrity. It's who you are when the lights go out and you're left alone with your conscience. You cannot hide from yourself.

Integrity is about being honest in your dealings with both others and yourself. Integrity concerns what people think about you when you are not around—your reputation. It's about how people perceive you, and what message you send to others about your character. Do you compose yourself with dignity? Have respect for yourself and others? Having integrity is about sending a message to your family, friends and coworkers that you are truthful and reliable. What you expect from others you should also expect from yourself.

Responsibility determines whether your life is more about cultivating victimhood or victory. Taking responsibility for your words, thoughts, and actions will change your life. Part of taking responsibility is releasing the poison in your heart: forgiveness. Forgive others who have done you wrong, and forgive yourself. When we drop our baggage, we're far more ready to take action. Forgiveness doesn't always come easy, I know. Nursing a grudge sometimes feels like its own reward. It's like picking at a scab, or always pressing on a bruise so it can't heal. When I was younger I believed my mother and stepfather had purely selfish motives for giving me up. I despised my mother for abandoning her blood son. Now, older and wiser, I consider my mother's actions in a somewhat different light. I can't time travel or read minds—but I ask myself, what if my interpretation was completely off base?

Maybe I was right, maybe I was wrong. But in either case, I was projecting motives on her, assuming a great deal about her intentions and reasoning. But I was a young boy. Did I really understand what it was all about? It's as likely as not that she knew she couldn't provide a healthy life for me, considering all the problems she had. And even if her motives were selfish, wasn't she really doing me a favor? Maybe people's intentions don't matter; it's what results from their actions that count. I would not be the man I am today if she'd kept me. I like the person I've become. Perhaps I would have hated the Derek Clark that "might have been."

I once heard this saying: "Do you know what the most flammable piece of wood is? The chip on your shoulder." As a teenager I was always ready to pick a fight. If you weren't for me, you were against me, and it was always easy for me to find an excuse to be mad at somebody. I was used to blaming others for my situation. It wasn't my fault—it was his, hers, or theirs. Sometimes I think I must have blamed everybody but the one-armed man. I figured everyone's big secret plan was always to hurt me in some way, to abuse my trust. If they were friends, I assumed they were just waiting for the perfect time to strike and make me feel like an idiot. I nurtured a healthy sense of victimhood.

I have had to learn and relearn that you can't believe everything you think. Every thought that comes into your mind must be honestly evaluated. Are you being objective, or is your judgment of a person, place, or thing being colored by some long-held prejudice? Does a particular thought or way of looking at things bring positivity or negativity into your life? Weigh it on the scale, is it sum negative or sum positive?

Make a commitment right now. Tell yourself that you are going to take responsibility. Tell yourself that you will not play the role of the victim. Get up, dust yourself off, and come back at it with new strength and wisdom. Why wait? Start answering to yourself today.

   Opportunity just means the chance to have exactly what you want in life. Opportunity may seem like a mysterious thing, a vague concept, or something that only happens to other people. But the good thing about opportunity is that it's always right there in front of you, ready for you to reach out and grab it! This is the true meaning of my sayings, Never Give Up and Never Limit Your Life. You must explore every opportunity that might contribute to the fulfillment of your dreams, career, education, and everything else. We live in a society that has carved out many paths to success, and there are usually people and institutions along the way that can give us a hand.

   Countless people who have done something great with their life did so simply because they had the courage to take a chance. They saw an opportunity and jumped right in. By taking risks, we are often led to opportunities we may never have imagined, or even dreamed of, had we been more timid. Possibilities open up like rosebuds at our touch. Sophocles said it perfectly when he wrote "Chance never helps those who do not help themselves." Opportunities are like nesting dolls: there is always a new one buried inside the old. So go for it, take a chance, and ROCK ON!

Choice is probably the biggest factor in whether you are going to live a fulfilling or miserable life. Everything in life revolves around a choice. We cannot stay still and are always in motion. We are either going forwards or backwards. It doesn't matter who you are; the wealthiest or the poorest person on Earth. It doesn't matter where you live; Lithuania or Tasmania or Kentucky. Your age doesn't matter; young, old, or inbetween. Who we are as individuals is just the sum of the choices we've made. Our first and most important choice concerns our attitude toward life. Be grateful for this time we've been given on Earth, and everything else will fall into place. Even the challenges can bring great happiness if we react positively.

Most of the time we know what the right choice is, but something in us occasionally opts to take the wrong path. There is a drive inside many of us to be self-destructive. Freud called it the death wish—some peculiar desire to shrug off the burden of doing right and just sinking into oblivion. Don't let this monkey climb up onto your back. Making the right choice is a courageous act. But thankfully, even bad choices are not without value. Every choice we make in life has something to teach us. We can't go back in time and correct our actions. But by making better choices today, we can rectify the consequences of poor decisions we've made in the past.

There are many people who are very intelligent, yet lack sharp instincts. Instinct is not based on reason, but it has its own reasons. I don't believe having brain-smarts is enough—you have to have gut-smarts. Instinct is that primal force within us that just knows what do in any situation. It is the fountainhead of will power and creativity. Some people strive to make decisions based on logic, but no decision is ever made by logic alone.

Have you ever heard of Buridan's Ass? It's a thought experiment. The idea is used to demonstrate that logic is not the ultimate source of our decisions. Imagine an ass—well, let's just say donkey—positioned an equal distance from two identical piles of oats. If the donkey were to choose based on logic alone, he'd be unable to make a decision, and would be stuck until he starved to death between the two twin piles of munchies. But the donkey does choose—he just goes for it. His instinct guides him to one decision, and he doesn't think, while he's munching on the oats—"Hmm, maybe those other oats would have been better!" He makes a call and moves on.

Whether marrying my wife at a young age or opening a business, all my most important decisions have been made by intuition. Being too logical can make us overly cautious. Logic dampens our instincts. Some people say that logic should always guide our instincts. But I say, let our instincts guide our logic. Logic would have told me to wait to marry my wife, or that there was far too much risk in starting my own company. But both have turned out to be two of the greatest decisions I ever made. Instinct is some deep part of ourselves. I call it our "soul's consciousness," because I don't know how else to think of it. It's a peculiar but powerful force, no doubt. Like the soul, it is intangible. It often has a mind of its own, and works in mysterious ways.

Knowledge is the key. You've heard that before—but how true it is! It's a key because it opens doors. Knowledge gives you options. Learning is growing—it's the human equivalent of the mighty oak or elm's striving to branch out and reach the sky. Always seek advice when making big decisions. One of my friends passed on some great wisdom to me, saying "Derek, when you want make a big decision, check with three of your smartest friends." Always make sure you have friends who are smarter than you. These are the people who will help you rise to their level. In high school I didn't hang out with the academic scholars; I mainly hung out with the academically challenged! Now I try to have friends who are smarter than me in areas where I am lacking knowledge. And I hope that I am a

90

useful friend in areas where I am more experienced than they are.

Knowledge is so important in helping catapult dreams into reality. But I also believe that knowledge should go hand-in-hand with imagination. Knowledge is always limited, whereas imagination is completely unlimited. But knowledge helps guide your imagination; it is the boatman who steers. Without the two working in tandem, it's hard to deliver something tangible to the world.

Imagine I wanted to become a professional songwriter. Well, I wouldn't be a very good one if I didn't learn about different types of music, notes, syncopation, tone, melody, timing, rests, and other aspects of music theory. I would probably end up writing songs nobody wanted to hear. Find out what somebody already occupied in your dream job had to learn. You may need special schooling, degrees, or skills. The more you exercise your intelligence and expand your knowledge, the more information you have to make the educated decisions that will impact your life.

Do not be afraid to ask questions! Ask away and be curious! Make sure you are taking in as much information as you can about different cultures, art, music, travel, education, religions, political views, foods, and everything else under the sun. With information comes understanding. If we had more people interested in gathering good information, we would have a lot less ignorance about each other and our differences. Everybody approaches the world a little differently. Find out which ways suit you and are beneficial. Choose which bits you want to apply in our own life. Knowledge is power—now go get you some!

So there you have it. When you look in the mirror, tempted to pick yourself apart because there is something about yourself you don't like, I want you to say out loud: "I ROCK!" Give yourself a little love. Look into your eyes and say it again: "I ROCK!" You won't be able to help feeling a little smile creeping onto your face. You know that you have a lot to offer this world. And while you're there at the mirror, say some other things to yourself. "I Like Myself! I Am Living This Life Now! I Am Grateful For What I Have, and I Respect Myself Because I ROCK!"

<u>Words and Identity</u>

You are like an unshaped stone or block of clay. Words give shape to our thoughts, and our thoughts shape the person we are. Words also color our perception of the world we live in. You've heard the phrase, "Sticks and stones can break my bones, but words will never hurt me." It's an admirable defense against insults, but the truth is that words indeed can hurt you. More so even than sticks and stones. You can recover from physical injury, but it can be much harder to recover from the words that fill your mind. You must be conscious of both the words you speak to yourself and the words others speak to you. It takes practice to be aware of what you're saying. Often words seem to just fly out of our mouths so fast we can't take hold of their source in our mind. But once you start being conscious of the words you use, it will become habit.

I once heard a great quote: "If you complain, there you will remain." People's thoughts can run a deep groove in their minds, until certain ways of thinking become habitual. Our mind runs down the well-worn groove; the path of least resistance. I call it Broken Record Syndrome. The same thing repeats over and over in your head, until you must forcibly move the needle down a new path of thinking. Words of negativity, self-doubt, and criticism seem to form these deep ruts much easier than words of consolation, confidence, and compliments. If you have a voice in your head that emphasizes your own limitations, you will come to think of yourself as limited. If you constantly think of yourself as a victim, you will develop a victim mentality. The victim voice is the voice that says you are not talented enough, that you're ugly, too short, and nobody likes you. "Poor you," the voice says, "poor, poor you."

Words can be like the links to a chain that holds your spirit captive. They can be like a sedative, making your spirit go dormant. But you can control what you think. Be the gatekeeper to your mind, and only allow good things to enter. When you look in the mirror, do you pick yourself apart? Point out all the flaws, zits, and scars?

96

Do you focus on how big your ears and nose are? Maybe you don't like the color of your eyes or your hair. We all have things about ourselves we'd like to change. But picking yourself apart brings negative energy into your heart and mind. Soon, you start to identify with the negative, with what you don't like about yourself instead of what you do.

Ask yourself if you are speaking words of faith or fear. Then step back and observe what comes your way. The more you talk about something, the more it comes to be your reality. If you look in the mirror every day and say, "I'm fat", chances are you'll stay overweight. But if you tell yourself you are a *skinny fat-burning machine*, you will attract the type of positive energy that inspires you to shed some pounds. You will take actions directly related to the words.

The first step I took toward living a more rewarding life was speaking the right kind of words. I spoke words that inspired great intentions, that brought out the best in me, and that produced encouraging thoughts. Did you know the words you speak and think with can be prophetic? They can completely change the quality of your life, for good or bad. When you speak negative words, words of pity and defeat, you are going to attract these negative forces into your life. When you speak positive words of faith and victory, you are going to attract that kind of power as well.

I used to have a secret identity. Instead of being "Super Man", I was "Pain Man". My defensive walls were always up, and nobody could see that I was dying inside. I was the walking wounded all throughout high school. I masked my pain with the identity I created. Everyone saw me as a clown and fighter. I was afraid to share my pain with anyone else. I kept it bottled up until I discovered I had a talent for rap, so I became a rapper. My name was Diamond, because a diamond shines and is unbreakable.

I could beat-box, I could spit the lyrics and flow. I was the D-I-A-M-O-N-D! I loved that I could express myself this way. Rap can have lyrics of vulnerability, while being expressed in an assertive way that disguises the message. Growing up in the

San Francisco Bay Area, I found many opportunities to express myself in competitions against others. I'd win and lose, but was always ready to go up against a new challenger.

Diamond is just one of the identities that has followed me around in my life. It is a true, authentic part of me, and I love sharing it with the crowds. Diamond is good for breaking stereotypes and shattering preconceptions about who I am supposed to be. It is a big surprise when Diamond comes out of the box, and he teaches people that you can't judge a book by its cover. You never know how other people might surprise you. More importantly, you never know how you might surprise yourself.

We have all been labeled by others at some point in our life. But the opinions of others don't have to warp our sense of self. People might label you based on your behaviors. They might call you a drunk, a druggie, or a quitter. Maybe you've even done things to justify their labels. But it doesn't matter if you've made poor choices! Mistakes are happenstance, incidental to our character. They are not who we are. Today is the day to move forward.

If you've been dishonest, it's time to right your wrongs and keep on keeping on. If you're making honest changes, and people insist on seeing you the same way, perhaps you need to forget about trying to show them you've changed. Find some other people. Let them into your heart so they can take a look around and see if they like what's there. If they don't, no biggie. Just move on. Someone will eventually. You will be evolving, forcing yourself to grow every time you let someone get to know you.

When I was married at age 23, I didn't even have a job. I got laid off literally days before the wedding. In fact, the night before the ceremony, my wife's maid of honor called her up very concerned to tell her that she shouldn't marry me because I was immature and wasn't employed. When my wife told me about the phone call, I couldn't believe it. My wife sure had a lot of faith in me. Needless to say, it was awkward the next day when looking at the maid of honor. We stayed our distance, but I guess I can't blame her for what she did. She was just another person who didn't have faith in me.

On the other hand, my wife had complete faith in me. Why else would she marry an unemployed man? I am here to tell you that we were living off of love. Soon my wife was also laid off from her job, only a month after we said "I do." We were both out of work, living off unemployment benefits, eating noodles and frozen vegetables with the occasional hotdog thrown in. The honeymoon marriage was short-lived, and now we were in the real world. It was a crazy time for us. We had lots of stress, arguments, and doubts about whether our marriage was even going to work. At one point we thought about calling it quits and going back home to our parents. But we had a meeting and decided we would be a team from that point on.

I finally found a job in sales and promised myself that I would never be broke again. With hard work I excelled at my new occupation, but I could never have done it without my wife's support and the WILL within me. I was determined to improve my situation, and with that determination I succeeded in providing a quality life for my wife and children. I was also able to pay for my wife to complete her schooling at a California State University. Things turned out wonderfully. But if my wife had paid attention to the label her friend was applying to me, we may never have been able to share the many wonderful years we have.

It all starts with what is inside your heart. Mold your identity in such a way that it works in tune with your behavior. It's time to start seeing yourself in a more positive manner, one that correlates more closely with the vision of yourself that you hold in your heart. I'm not suggesting you change your identity on the fly. You need something deeper and longer lasting. Identity runs deep: you may have to build your new self from the ground up. With the proper effort, though, you can become the person you've always wanted to become.

WILL is the Way

Philosophers and theologians have debated for millennia what the nature of free will is, or if it even exists. It's one of those deep philosophical questions that will never be decided to any one side's satisfaction. But there have been those who find a compromise: they say that, even if we do not have free will, we should always act as if we do. It becomes a kind of faith. It feels like free will—and as the saying goes, if it walks like a duck, quacks like a duck, and looks like a duck, it's probably a duck.

I fall firmly on the side of those who profess free will. Determination can change your life forever. When we are the captains of our own boats, there's no telling what port we might find ourselves mooring in. There is a four-letter word that over time and through frequent use has been woven into the fabric of my soul, and that word is WILL. The willpower to succeed is no easy task. But again we go back to purpose. Once we have purpose, a destination towards which we set our course, self-determination becomes the wind in our sails. It all starts with a belief that we can be masters of our fate.

Purpose is a seed planted deep within you. When you water that seed and encourage it to grow, energy is produced. Energy wants to be spent. It creates motion and motion creates action. Action creates results, results create achievement, and achievement creates self-confidence. Self-confidence is a mindset that reinforces the knowledge that you can and WILL achieve anything you set your mind to.

I have always had the WILL to take action and the WILL to never give up. This word has given me unyielding strength to conquer all the challenges I've encountered. However, willpower can sometimes seem like a vague concept. We all know it is some indefinable force within that drives us, pushing us relentlessly through the obstacles in our way. But in order to make it something easier to get ahold of, I came up with an acronym for WILL. It is not the definition of will, but rather, an expression of it.

Whatever
Is
Lacking,
Learn!

You have heard the phrase, where there's
a will there's a way. But the formula works
in reverse. Where there's a way, there's a
will. Will is good, but will is not conscious.
It is a primal force that knows nothing of the
world. We have to direct this natural energy,
and feed it knowledge. If a goal seems
beyond our reach because we simply don't
know how to do something, or where to get
started, learn whatever you can about the
destination you wish to arrive at. The will
gets you there, but it has to be channeled and
focused so that its vitality is not dispersed
willy-nilly.

I like the word will. But there are two
words that, when used together, really get
under my skin. They are "I" and "can't." I
can't. If you ever find yourself in a situation
where you're tempted to give up, think of
that children's story *The Little Engine That
Could.* I'm not sure parents even read it to

their children any more, but I hope they do. I remember it being a great inspiration, not only as a child, but as an adolescent and young adult. Even now, if you want the truth. Sure, it's kind of an inside joke between me, myself, and I. But I'm not kidding about the many times I've found myself in a fix and, needing a dose of can-do attitude, discovered that little choo-choo train popping into my head. Remember how he goaded himself on: "I think I can, I think I can, I think I can." Repeat it. Let it be your mantra and marching cadence. I can do this. I can make this happen. I can win. Just the words "I can" will empower you. Only the tough-minded get to the places that are worth going.

There are those who say, "I would have done something with my life if I had more time." Then there are those who say, "I could have been something if I had only applied myself." Or how about the ones who say, "I should have devoted more time to my dreams." Well, Woulda-Coulda-Shoulda— but most of all, SHOULDA NEVER GIVEN UP!!!!

"I've missed over 9,000 shots in my career. I've lost almost 300 games. 26 times I've been trusted to take the game-winning shot...and missed. I've failed over and over and over again in my life. And that is why I succeed." -- Michael Jordan

Be Valuable to Your Company

Companies and their employees are a team, and both company and employee should remember this. The strength of a company is built upon the pride of its employees. I believe in incentives and rewards. It drives up employee morale. People should be rewarded for their successes and recognized for doing an outstanding job. There are many employees who are loyal to their company, but the company is not always loyal to them. This is one sure way a business sows the seeds of its own failure. However, it's a two-way street. Employees have to demonstrate loyalty to the company. A company has to know that you've taken ownership of the job, and that you're not just there to take up space and fill time. It's a running joke in the business world that many employees do just enough to not get fired. You have to go beyond this, and bring your energy and enthusiasm to go the extra mile. When you feel yourself slacking off, think of what

Vince Lombardi said: "If you aren't fired with enthusiasm, you will be fired with enthusiasm."

Different personalities can have different strengths. Employers already know this well. The crabby guy who everyone wants to avoid may be brilliant at writing computer code. Perhaps he is an anti-social introvert, but he brings a lot of value to the company. But a person like this will most likely not climb the company's ladder. He is respected for getting his job done, but if you're like me, you want positive people in leadership positions in order to move the company in a positive direction. You simply must have the right attitude and necessary social skills if you want to become management. If our hypothetical grump was instead the kind of person who reached out and helped others, he'd be the perfect employee. Think about what kind of energy you bring to the workplace. It's about both skills and attitude.

Nobody's job is secure, so always continue sharpening your skills. Do not get complacent or become stagnant. We all answer to someone. Even the President of Nike, McDonalds, Macy's and The Septic Cleaner answer not only to stockholders, but to the market. If they cannot make a product that will fill the need of the buyer, they will soon be out of business. The same goes for you. If you do not continue to update your skills and build knowledge about your industry, you could be on the outs. It's a lot easier getting better at what we do than trying to get hired at a new business, and trying to prove all over again that we have what it takes to be a great hire.

Don't be afraid to have meetings with your employer, and ask questions about how you are doing and where you can improve. Let him or her know you are working on developing your skills and want to be ahead of the game. You want the boss to know you can be counted on, that you want to be a team player and a leader, and that you want to bring value to the company. This will keep you at the forefront of your boss's mind when it comes time to promote someone. It isn't enough to simply say it though; actions must match your words. Don't just talk the talk, walk the walk.

Research how you can improve yourself. Go back to school if need be, get additional training, or work on familiarizing yourself with the software programs your company uses. Better yet, become an expert in these softwares. Many people only know the basics of computer programs, so you will stand out if you know the ins and outs. Ask to be trained for different positions, in case the company needs a back up. We all have professional weaknesses, and we need to be real about them. If you can only type 40 words per minute, it's time to hit the typing trainer. If you have been intimidated about a new software program, dive right in and practice using it. Programs can be frustrating, and people often give up learning them immediately. But every program has either an online tutorial or a book. Nobody is born knowing Excel, Publisher, or Powerpoint. This is your job— take it seriously and take pride in it. Again, it's a whole lot easier to dive in and learn what needs learning than to walk into the unemployment office and dive into their paperwork. Especially while wishing all the while that you would have paid more attention to developing yourself when you still had the chance.

Make some goals right now and find out how you can perform at your highest level. Start networking with your peers and top people. Learn from those on the top so that you can rise to the top. You can always find a mentor or a trainer willing to spend time helping you hone your skills. Remember to be grateful for their time. Go to seminars and conventions, and read books and magazines about your industry. There is always something new to learn. If you think you know all there is to know, you're certainly mistaken. Besides, every day brings new changes, so do what you can to stay abreast of these.

SALES!!!
Live Beyond Limits

"Here's the rock, paper, scissors of selling: Relationship is more powerful than price. Relationship is more powerful than delivery. Relationship is more powerful than quality. Relationship is more powerful than service." Jeffrey Gitomer

I don't think anyone who knew me when I was young would have predicted I'd be the founder of several successful companies. Even I probably would have been a little skeptical if some time-traveling fellow from the future had come and laid the news on me. I would have asked him, "You sure you have the right Derek Clark?" Then I would have asked, "Just what are you smoking, again?" Now, a good many years after my first major business venture, I admit there must have been some trait present in young Derek Clark, some disposition that would grow like an acorn into an oak, turning the boy I was into the man I am.

So every once in a while I take a moment to go over my life, combing my memories for clues, asking myself where it all sprang from. What was the drive? Where was the entrepreneurial seed? What in my young spirit led me to where I am today? In the final analysis, I decided it all came from a very unexpected place: my bad attitude.

My foster parents will tell you: "Derek had no fear." Sometimes they'll tell you with a smile, sometimes with a frown. I caused them a lot of worry and headaches. Sure, I could be fearless, but not always in healthy ways. Though on the whole I always tried to be a good person, I was troubled. I had a lot of anger buried deep down inside me, and it wasn't expressed through depression and melancholy. I was often aggressive and quick to act out. I didn't think anybody could be trusted. It all went back to my mother giving me up. If she could throw me to the wolves, what on earth could stop anybody else from doing the same?

The time I spent bouncing from foster family to foster family imprinted a certain uneasiness on me, and insecurities concerning my worth as a human being. Even during those years when I was settled and wonderfully happy with my foster family, it would often come to my mind that I wasn't with my real family. Maybe it was senseless—I have no doubt growing up with my foster family was far healthier than it would have been spending my formative years with my biological one; but these feelings creep into our minds.

Always tall for my age, I was never afraid to tell someone off, get into a fight, or let some poor person know I broke their special something. I had little respect for authority, regardless of who was wielding it. It could be an older and bigger kid, a school official, a church elder, or whoever else got in my way. Now of course I regret that I ever hurt anybody, and see that my attitude was completely out of bounds. I think I have could have channeled that energy toward more constructive ends. Yet there was something about my standoffish attitude— this feeling that I was pitted against the world—that allowed me to see things as an outsider and gain an individualistic perspective.

A certain disregard for the opinions of others as a boy became a willingness to experience new things for myself and ignore naysayers. I am by no means suggesting that people be rude or angry, and would never encourage that attitude in my own children or suggest others cultivate it in theirs. My attitude was the result of being emotionally damaged. But every negative behavior can be twisted into a positive, depending on the context and how it is expressed.

Stubbornness in the boy can mean having firm principles as a man. Arrogance becomes confidence; foolhardiness becomes comfort with risk; rudeness becomes the capacity for honesty and the emotional strength to wear one's heart on their sleeve. We shouldn't tolerate negative behaviors in the young or in ourselves, but with a little tweaking, these behaviors can be the foundation for the positive attributes that aid us in our quest for success.

It was while I was still in elementary school that I learned the art of a good sell. It's an old platitude of the business world that if you want to be a success, you must first find a need and then go about filling it. Sometimes this need in the market will be obvious: people want faster computers, televisions with clearer pictures, and food that is both healthy and tasty. Other times, we might have to look to ourselves and ask: what is it I wish I had? What would make my life more enjoyable, convenient, or satisfying?

Looking around myself at eight years old, I saw that I was surrounded by little kids just like me. It didn't take any great leaps of imagination to zero in on what kids tend to like more than anything else in the world: sugar! I liked candy, and if my target demographic was anything like me, I knew they'd want it too. What were gold and silver, stocks and bonds, to children in northern California? They meant nothing. But a Snickers bar, a bag of M&M's, or a roll of Now & Laters—ah, well, that was currency indeed!

So in that child's brain of mine I concocted what you might call a rudimentary business plan. It wasn't General Electric, but for a kid my age I think it was pretty sharp. I was going to turn a profit one way or another, and my product was going to be candy. But how? My first stumbling block was in scheduling. I had to be in school early in the morning, and then back home right after the three o'clock bell rang to do my homework and chores. Where was I going to find time to purchase my product? No way were my parents going to support me in some off-the-wall business scheme, using my school chums as my clientele. Especially not when I was going to sell them something their parents wouldn't want them to have.

It quickly became clear that the only time I had to burn was the time I was at school. Frankly, I wasn't the best student in the world, and I figured my teachers wouldn't miss me too terribly much. I made my first big move one day. Who knows, perhaps it was the day that sealed my fate as a future businessman. The bus dropped me off in front of our school. Instead of going in through the big double doors, I had a friend create a diversion. While he started screaming maniacally and waving his arms, I ducked around behind the bus and took off running across the parking lot. Once I was off school grounds and safely away from the prying eyes of teachers, I hit a side road. Turning up the sharp upward hill back towards town, I trotted off towards the candy shop.

The candy shop was an odd one. It was run out of a house by an elderly couple. There in the living room were racks and racks of everything a young boy or girl dreams of. To this day I'm not sure why it was there or how it came to be, but I wasn't about to question my good luck. I'd rush in with the money I'd saved from chores and gather up whatever I could in a hurry. I'd get back to school just in time for the first recess period and "set up shop" in some quiet corner of the school. I'd bring out the candy and sell it to the highest bidder.

The operation quickly grew into a full-on racket. I enlisted a couple other "employees," and we began ditching school at lunch. One of my cohorts would create distractions at the tetherball or basketball court, while another buddy and I would climb over the back gate, running as fast as we could towards town so we could make it back before the bell rang. We'd buy Pixie Stix and Now-&-Laters for a nickel a piece, and sell them for a quarter at a 400% profit.

This was one of my first experiences learning how to deal with money and filling a need in a market. In retrospect, I see that all I really did was look for an opportunity and took a risk in order to turn a profit. Perhaps the reward wasn't worth the risk. I could have been suspended, run over by a car, or even kidnapped. Risk must be calculated, in business and in life, but making money always entails going out on a limb in some way. Long gone are my days of trying to make a quarter out of five cents, but the principle is still the same: fill a need, turn a profit, and become a lean, green, money-making machine. Going from selling candy in the schoolyard to becoming a top salesperson in your field is not as great a leap as you might think.

Sales is sales is sales. If you can sell one thing successfully, you can sell anything. It's all about having the proper outlook and filling a need. What is the void in people's life, and how can you as a salesperson make their life a little better? Of course we've all heard of the proverbial salesman who could sell ice to Eskimos, but I've also heard salespeople say, "I could sell anything, even my fingernail clippings!" To that I say, "Okay, just try it!" Where is the need for somebody's clipped fingernails? It must be a very niche market indeed.

To me, selling isn't about manipulating buyers or pulling the wool over their eyes. It's not about wearing the customer down or strong-arming a possible purchaser. Sure, there is "a sucker born every minute," but it's this attitude that sometimes gives sales a bad name. Customers or clients often have a standoffish or suspicious attitude towards salespeople, because they have a deep-seated sense that the salesperson is going to try and pawn off some product or service that they don't need and is no good for them anyway. They're worried about being swindled. This dynamic is unfortunate, and in no way should it exist in a sales relationship. Sales should be all about presenting a product or service that makes a client's eyes light up. They should look at your offerings, and say, "Man, I need that."

Let's go back to fingernail clippings. Nobody would buy them because there's no inherent value in them. In order to sell them you'd have to be a con artist, fabricating value where in reality there is none. But suppose you're trying to sell Elvis' fingernail clippings. Well then you might have an in-demand product! Many people have the desire or need to feel they own something close to Elvis, and his fingernail clippings may just fill that need.

Since the need is real, and not simply created or fabricated, you're doing the buyer a service by delivering a product that makes them happier than they would have been without it. Sure, we might smirk about somebody wanting Elvis' fingernails, but that doesn't mean the need isn't there to begin with. There are many strange markets in this world, and it's not a salesperson's business to judge.

There are a million and one books on sales. If you're like me and read business and self-improvement books, I'm sure you've heard it all. There are always new strategies sales strategies being put forth, new developments in sales processes, and step-by-step instructions for "closing the deal." It's my belief that this is all dross, and innovation for its own sake. For me, successful salesmanship comes down to some basic principles that I am going to share. These principles are all you need to know in order to have tremendous success. I've always applied them, and they have never failed me.

First and foremost, sales is all about the right attitude. You must not be afraid to hear a "No." It's not the end of the world. Many people don't do well in the industry because they have a great fear of rejection. They sometimes feel a "no" is a rejection of them personally. It isn't. There are many variables that can end a sale. Buyers will test you with limited time, be unwilling to meet with you, put you down, cancel purchases, back out at the last minute, and seek out a competitor who will undercut you at the last minute.

Typically sales is about helping somebody feel better about buying something they know they already want, and sometimes a product or service is simply not a good fit for a particular buyer. That doesn't mean you don't try, but be willing to accept defeat. Selling is about being comfortable with discomfort. You are going to hear a thousand and one no's, but great salespeople don't care what others think. They have a goal and they believe in their product. It's a numbers game, so don't let "the one that got away" sway your confidence.

As I said before, sales is not about deception. Just be honest and work hard! Honesty will pay off big time in the long run. Business is based on relationships, and word gets around fast concerning what type of dealer you are. You may have played fast and loose with the truth and made a sale, but one deal does not make a great businessman, just like one slam-dunk in basketball doesn't make you Michael Jordan. You have to think about the long term and repeat business. Don't turn off a customer by delivering them a product that doesn't match up to how you sold it. You want to under-promise and over-deliver, not over-promise and under-deliver.

Before you make a sales call, know everything you can about your product, your competition, and your buyer. Know what you're selling in and out, so you can share all of its advantages. Many people have only a superficial knowledge of their product. When the buyer raises suspicion or opposition, or even just asks a question, the salesperson chokes and stumbles on their words, saying: "I need to get back to you."

This means you haven't done your research, and even if you're up to speed in most other respects, and an honest broker besides, the customer may lose faith in the deal. That said, it's always better to be up front about something you aren't sure of. A client will be much happier with an honest "I don't know" than they will with a line of bull that is exposed as such later on down the road. It's much harder to recover from a lie than it is a little ignorance or gap in your knowledge.

If you sincerely believe in your product, others will see value in it too. Human beings are hardwired to pick up on the subtlest body language and facial cues, and even the most accomplished liars will reveal their fibs on their faces or the tone of their voice. A buyer, even if only at a subconscious level, will note the slightest hesitation or uncertainty. Something will nag at them, preventing them from having complete faith in the exchange. I am serious about this: be prepared.

One way to get to know your product, and deal with issues that may come up concerning it, is role-play. I can't recommend it enough. If available, seek out the best salesperson in your company, and see if they won't go a few rounds practicing different scenarios with you. Take them out for lunch. Hang around with them. Pick up on their energy. Watch how they communicate on the phone. Don't be afraid to ask questions. When role-playing, try to come up with every possible objection to your product or your pricing. Come up with answers to any potential questions or concerns. Your fellow role-player doesn't have to come at you like a bully, but it isn't terribly helpful if they don't challenge you to find the best responses to difficult questions.

Just as you need to build trust with your significant other, you must build trust with your clients. It's all about listening. It's interesting that the word "listen" is composed of the exact same letters as the word "silent". Listening is about taking in what the other person wants to talk about. You must do it without automatically trying to offer solutions or advice. First listen, then ask questions and get clarification. Be genuine, and don't hesitate to praise them for their openness. Once you fully understand what their needs are, you can explain how your product or service answers their need.

Of all the reasons a sale falls through, the one best and perhaps most easily avoided is a personality clash between seller and buyer. Being too pushy up front or arrogant will not get you where you want to go. I have had many reps from many different companies call on me to give them business. Even if I liked the product they were selling, I can tell you without a doubt that the ones who were kind, respectful and conscientious of my time were far more likely to get my business.

You want everything on the table so that nothing is misinterpreted. One bad move can ruin a business relationship forever; but a good experience can lead to lifetime partnerships. Never commit to something you cannot deliver on, and don't spread yourself so thin that your clients suffer or feel they're being unattended. Make sure your support team double-checks everything to head off any problems that might arise from a deal too hastily made.

You want to wow your clients. When you deliver the goods, buyers will talk about you and referrals will come. When you do a great job, it won't feel improper to ask for referrals from people they think would benefit from your product or service. Referrals are the life-blood of your business.

Great sales are made from word of mouth, and when you've got a good reputation potential buyers are already sold on you. Half the work is already done! I love my cheerleaders because they continue to talk highly of me and share my products with everyone else.

Like yourself, and don't be afraid to close the sale when it feels like the right time. Go into the sale fully expecting to make it happen. Just as the client will pick up on deception, they will also pick up on your confidence. Don't be pushy, and refuse to back off even after you've received a firm "no." There's no need to embarrass yourself over a no. Move on. The person who said no this time may come back to you in the future, but that is far less likely if you make a big production out of their turning you down. Your product will not fill everybody's needs. There is no way that one company can capitalize on every household. Competition between similar products from different brands is a fundamental of our economy. You must think about what niche your products fits, and go after those who exist in that niche.

Something that is very practical and will take your business to the next level is data-basing. Information is gold in business; it is your past, present, and future. Keeping good records is as important for the large corporation as the small business. I use Microsoft Access and Act, but there are many different software programs that will help you keep an informative database. You don't have to push networking or business chat on everybody you encounter at a cocktail party or barbecue, but it's good to keep in mind that every person you come in contact with is a potential client. If they're not, they will almost certainly know of somebody who is. Put yourself out there. Let people know what line of work you are in and what you have to offer. Serendipity is part of business. It often happens that chance encounters bring us into contact with clients who need our services.

You can generally tailor your software with different categories. These are the ones I use and find most helpful when entering a new contact. First, I put the date I first met him or her. Their name, address, county, email address, website, phone number, what products they use, and what product I can try to sell them on. Lastly, I fill out their profile by listing any hobbies or interests they have and may have spoken about. Usually there is a lot about golfing, fishing, traveling, cars, wine, music, books, and family. It's good to know what interests your clients have. When you come across an article related to their interests, email or cut it out and mail it to them, with a note saying, "I thought you'd be interested in this because of your passion for_____." It helps to establish what you might call a business friendship. This doesn't mean you're simply putting on the appearance of caring. You should be genuinely interested in your business contacts, as they are important relationships in your life.

I also code each prospect according to a hot/cold category. Are they a hot, warm, or cold lead? I will also make notes about where I met this person and how. Was it at a party, barbeque, or the supermarket? What were the circumstances under which I met them? I also list who might have put me in contact with them and why. Was it a referral? Drop-in? Cold call or a call-in? Or perhaps they came to me through my marketing or advertising efforts. Once the contact is in, the work is not done. I will always have a conversation log of any conversations we might have had, and update my records every time we communicate. I note the date I sent them an email, made a phone call or had mail correspondence, and summarize the nature of the conversation so that I know where we left off and where we might be headed.

Every time you meet someone, make them feel like a million bucks. Don't be an insincere flatterer, but don't be afraid to honestly praise their successes. Opportunities come when you help others feel better about themselves. Remember that negativity can suck the life out of a business meeting, but positivity charges it up so that both parties feel excited about the possibilities.

I also highly recommend sending handwritten cards to each person you've met, along with your business card. Let them know it was nice to meet them and that you'd appreciate it if they let others know of your services. I usually say something like, "Don't keep me a secret to your friends, family and co-workers!" Some people think this is too forward, or artificial, or imposing. But trust me, people who do business both expect this and desire it. If you're going to be in business you cannot be a wallflower. If nobody knows you're game to work deals, how do you expect things to happen? People in business are never shy about doing a little networking.

I am a fan of old school qualities. Even in the age of instant digital communications, people still want the human touch. So many people just send out mass emails nowadays that when you receive an actual card actually handwritten by an actual human, it's like a refreshing breeze. Even if it only seems like a small thing, it's heartening that somebody took a second from the hustle and bustle of life to give you that extra bit of attention. I can't tell you how many times I've checked the ink on a business letter to see if the signature was handwritten or just printed. Even better, if somebody took the time to write me a handwritten letter, they go right to the top. It means that I wasn't just a faceless number, and that they are sincere about wanting to build a business relationship with me.

I used to send out thousands of letters at a time, but would make sure to sign each one personally. I'd create a letter in Microsoft Word and merge it with Access to auto-populate the names and addresses, but would afterward spend a few nights quickly signing my autograph on each one while watching TV. I always used blue ink and made sure my signature touched the closing salutation, whether it was sincerely or best regards. Sure, my hand cramped up quite a bit, but that's a small price to pay for the personal touch.

Start Your Own Business?

Perhaps a book on professional success by an entrepreneur would not be complete without a chapter on entrepreneurship. One of these days I will write a book exclusively on the topic. For now, I only want to touch on the matter. Many people dream of starting a company and being their own boss. However, this desire will only take you so far. Having your own business means complete dedication.

Eventually, you may be able to sell your business or set it up so that it runs itself and you are mostly generating passive income. In the beginning though, you will have to find a way to completely incorporate your work life into your personal life, until its woven together into a complete fabric. It can be difficult to imagine how much work it is to run a company you've founded. It can be a tremendously rewarding experience, but you have to be sure you are in it to win it, and willing to accept that the buck will stop with you.

When it became time for me to start my own company, I was already in the industry I wanted to be in. It was much easier because I knew a lot about the business. If you want to start a business in an entirely different field than the one you are currently in, go for it. But don't neglect doing the research. When you step out on a limb you want to make sure you have all the facts concerning your new venture.

If you're going to take a risk, you want it to be an informed decision. Weigh the risks. Consider the consequences. There will be new stresses on you, mentally and financially. Many companies fail within the first two years. You have to make sure you are filling a consumer need, and then position yourself differently than your competitors so that you stand out. A unique product at the right price is the key to a new company's success.

In my case, I did a thorough evaluation of the costs. I needed to rent office space, hire employees, and market my company. I consulted designers on creating a logo, letterhead, business cards, advertising, and internet presence. It was going to cost a pretty penny. In additional to financial resources, I needed emotional and spiritual resources. This is where your personal relationships come into play. Consult the people in your life. It helps to have somebody who will boost your morale, and who is willing to shoulder the risk with you. When I told my wife I wanted to go into business for myself, she did not hesitate to offer her support. She has always been my greatest cheerleader in all of my many ventures, adventures, and misadventures.

There are immediate pitfalls to avoid immediately after starting your business. You have to know where to spend your money in order to get the biggest rate of return on it. You have to build your clientele from the ground up. The first thing I did was send out personalized letters to all of my previous clients, letting them know the exciting news. I explained how my company and team of employees were going to help them with their needs. I advertised locally so that I would be one of the go-to names in a competitive market. I had to be targeted with my marketing budget, and make sure I didn't blow all of my money on one big advertising campaign. I built slowly and didn't overextend myself, all the while setting aside funds dedicated to bringing in new business.

Positive thinking is a must, but you must also be practical in order to make a new company work. You need a product people truly want and a great support team. Everything comes down to numbers and percentages. Don't be sentimental about your business; be analytical. You are looking for Return On Investment, period. Even if what you have is a splendid idea in theory, you have to listen to the numbers. They do not lie to flatter your ego. If the number projections aren't good, you need to consider letting your business go or reformulating your business strategy. If you are not good with money, hire somebody who has the expertise to help you make financial decisions.

Even if you have a great idea and a solid business plan, remember that the economy is what controls business. Booms and busts, recessions and inflation will dictate when, where, how, and to whom you market your product. Be flexible. What worked before may not work in the current market. Try to bend with the storm, like a palm tree in a hurricane. Bend but don't break; when the winds settle and you bounce back, you may just be stronger due to the adversity.

Many companies come through hard times leaner and meaner than they were before. But in the end, sometimes you just have to know when to quit and move ahead with something else before it totally drowns you. Think of that old Kenny Rogers song, "The Gambler". "You gotta know when to hold 'em, know when to fold 'em, know when to walk away, know when to run." This doesn't mean you don't get back on the horse and ride. It just means that it may be time to buy a different horse.

Imagination and Dreams

I love how Walt Disney responded to some people who said, "Think outside the box." He replied, "No! Don't think outside the box! Once you say that, you've established that there is a box." Walt Disney never acknowledged limits to the imagination, and he turned his fantasies into an inspiring reality. If you can dream it, you can do it. An active imagination is the key to happiness.

If we were all curious and inventive like a child, eager to explore the realms of our mind and act upon the magic we find there, the world would be a lot better place. It would be a lot more fun too. Imagination is in essential in so many different ways, it's hard to overemphasize how important it is. From inventions to problem-solving, to inspiring faith and putting a smile on a sad person's face, imaginative vision is one of our greatest assets as human beings.

Imagination is a potent force. And when mixed with courageous action, it can change the world. When I want to be mindful of imagination's immense potential, I don't have to go far. All I do is look at the everyday objects surrounding me. It's easy to take commonplace items for granted—they're easy to come by and we see them all the time. But remember, at one time literally none of the useful things around us existed. They could hardly even be dreamt of.

Many years ago, some Brazilian authorities and anthropologists flew a handful of elders from an isolated rain forest tribe to Rio de Janeiro. The men literally peed themselves when they beheld a modern metropolis. Don't laugh; you certainly would have had the same response. These men were just like us, only they came from a place that was frozen in time. The technological innovations we take for granted were so far beyond their frame of reference, the experience was overwhelming.

Look around you and count the miracles. Electricity was discovered, harnessed, controlled, and distributed to my home so I can merely flip a switch and the lights go on—that my friends is miracle! Central heating, power grids, gasoline, toilets, phones, faxes, computers, pencils and artificial hearts. All these seemingly disparate technologies have one thing in common: the people who devised them never quit. It was their life's purpose to think creatively and break through the walls of the infamous "box." These inventors were all amazing, and truly rock! They shared one common motto: Never Give Up! If anybody thinks imagination doesn't affect the world, you need only point them to a post-it note or a refrigerator. If they laugh, it's only because they've become desensitized to the wonders they see every day.

Don't be afraid to let your mind go off into flights of fancy. Practice makes perfect – why not spend a few minutes daydreaming every day? I know so many people who are self-conscious about creating. They don't want to write, paint, make music, or dream up original ideas—they think none of these pastimes are for them. But we are all blessed with the creative ability. It may be a weathered old chestnut by now, but Edison's saying that genius is one percent inspiration and ninety-nine percent perspiration was right on the mark. Nobody starts off a Mozart or a Van Gogh. It takes practice and years of honing skills and refining one's individual vision. Everyone starts at square one, but with dedication we move to square two, three, four, and beyond.

If you are inspired to create or invent something, you must find a way to bring it to life. Be a builder, not just a dreamer. Every amazing project once started as a "mere" dream, and may have seemed impossible. The determination of individuals and groups has shown, however, that what seems impossible can be accomplished with the right amount of effort. There will always be nay-sayers in the world; people who tell you it can't be done, or whose first reaction to some idea is to scrunch their face up skeptically and say, "Impossible!" Ignore them. You have a legion of yes-sayers to look up to.

I have no doubt that everyone who has introduced something new and fantastic to the world had at least one person encouraging them to throw in the towel and let their dreams wither away into dust. Do you really think these "nattering nabobs of negativity" are the types of people who make history?

Aside from others, you cannot let that little voice in your head tell you that you're not good enough. Shut it up! The worst critic in our lives is all too often ourselves. Be careful how you speak to yourself. You may just talk yourself out of a great discovery, job, partner, spouse, education, or experience. And don't lose heart if you feel alone with your dreams and aspirations. It's great if we have the support of peers and loved ones, but this support network does not exist for everyone. Your dreams may isolate you to some degree. That is when you must remember that many prominent creators labored in solitude, or didn't receive immediate acknowledgment for their efforts. Fulfilling your life's purpose is a goal in itself, and whether there are ready accolades or not, at least you'll know you are being true to yourself.

Albert Einstein once said that "there are only two ways to live your life. One is as though nothing is a miracle and the other is as though everything is a miracle."

A question I get a lot is "How do I make my dream happen?" I tell them to never quit going for it. Stay focused, passionate, consistent and persistent. Learn from your mistakes and apply a different approach so that you can always have many tentacles stretched out and many irons in the fire.

At some point in your life you no doubt had a dream. Maybe it was to be a doctor, an astronaut, professional athlete, race-car driver, artist, President of the United States, or rock star. Even if you don't have a dream right now, you did when you were a child, because every child dreams. Even as adults, we dream. It may be a dream of getting out of an impoverished area, getting a better job, or being rich. Everything is attainable if you focus on what you want and take the action to move towards that goal. Everything is motion, you are either moving forwards or backwards. There is no standing still. When you stand still, you are not moving forward, and if you are not moving forward you are going backwards. Set your sights on the stars, not the sewage.

Go back in your mind and remember what you were like when you were seven. Recall how free from responsibilities you were, how you got along with everyone and had love in your heart. There didn't seem to be so many worries, and the worries we did have seem trivial now that we are older. Children find magic in everything. Emulate this child you once were, and this child will set your mind free. Even if your dream appears ridiculous, be ridiculous in equal measure by believing in it. Silliness is not silly. It lightens our hearts, and forces us question why we take life so seriously at times. Where there is laughter and goofiness, there is the energy required to make dreams come true.

Losing our ability to dream doesn't mean that we have simply become mature and put aside childish things. It means the world has grinded us down into a husk. As the years pass on, we become more serious and we get grumpier by increments. We rarely have time to think of ourselves, and the opportunities for a good laugh are fewer and far between. You become a complainer, and all too eager to plan pity-parties. What has helped me overcome this grumpy old man's attitude is simply becoming like a child, and not being self-conscious about being a goofball. Laugh, laugh and laugh! Laugh until your sides split.

Make sure you are around children as often as possible. They will teach you a great deal; the kinds of lessons you cannot pick up from other adults. See them as they are, before the world starts squashing their spirit and stuffing them into a cramped box. Sure, we all know that kids can be mean, temperamental, and demanding. But even during their worst behavior, or in the midst of their most exasperating moods, there is an innocence and naiveté that we adults have lost. We have lost our sense of wonder. I have four children, and I have always done my best to encourage their imagination.

They want to write adventure books, so I say do it! They want to play music, so I say do it! They want to laugh and play and be curious—so what do I tell them? DO IT!

Many people who know me know I have a big personality. I like to laugh and joke around. I am a big dreamer. Dreams are for both young and old alike. Age doesn't matter. What matters is the youthfulness of heart and mind. Grandma Moses did not even start painting until she was in her seventies. An advanced age does not mean you should worry about trying something completely new or different. Just in the past few years, I have written five books and produced dozens of songs that are available all over the internet. Don't waste your time sitting on the couch drinking and gorging on Cheetos while watching trash TV. Time slips by. Five years from now I will have even more books and songs to show for my time—ask yourself what you will have to show for *your* time in five years?

In Summary

This chapter is about pulling it all together. So many people are big crybabies. They cry when life is going good, and they cry when it's going bad. If you find yourself freaking out about something, take a deep breath and step back from your problems and gain a little perspective. We live in a land of opportunity. Our birthright just for being born in the United States is to have every chance to become what we want. So what if you can't buy that $150 pair of jeans or a luxury car; it's nothing to worry about. We all have been wronged at some point in our lives. People usually spend more energy dwelling on their past than they do planning for their terrific future. Get to work on where you're going, and leave the past where it belongs: in the past. One of my favorite sayings is, "Focus on where you are going to, not what you are going through."

There are so many people in this world who are suffering in the most extreme ways. They may have a life-threatening disease, or be homeless, or living in a Third World country that lacks enough food, clean water and adequate shelter. All around the world, millions—even billions—live under despotic regimes that stifle free speech, innovation, and economic opportunity. But I promise you, they are still able to laugh and smile. I've known many world-travelers. Time and time again there is one counter-intuitive impression that sticks with them all: some of the world's poorest seem like the world's happiest.

This is not to be naïve and romanticize poverty, especially the kinds of extreme poverty that breed sickness and misery. It is not poverty that makes these people happy, so much as a closeness to the Earth and familiarity with the joys of daily life. There is no time for self-pity, and they aren't obsessed with "keeping up with the Jones". It is something we in the West become too easily disconnected from. These people inspire the strength in me to keep moving forward and check myself when complaining about my own trials and tribulations.

Sometimes your purpose in life finds you, not the other way around. If somebody had told me a few years ago that I would be the author of five books and an international inspirational speaker, I would have asked what mental institution they escaped from. How foolish I would have been! The river that is your life flows free, and has a way of changing direction and overflowing its banks. When you are motivated and doing your best, more and different opportunities come your way. When you have complete faith in your abilities and you know, I mean *really know*, that you are going places, you begin to understand that nothing can stop you from achieving the success you were meant to have.

I have always been a person who tries. Sure, there were times I wanted to give up, to run away from the mounting challenges that come with any effort to try something unprecedented. Yes, I have failed and failed and failed. I have gone forward, backwards, and sideways. But I never got so sidetracked I lost sight of the main thing: keep doing your thing! Keep on trucking! I've said it before and I'll say it again: you never fail until you stop trying. These are not just the words on some inspirational poster. They are a refreshing and invigorating way to reconceive failure. Namely, that failure doesn't even exist as long as you stick to it.

The only real secret to success is determination. I have gone places because I was determined to. Just ask Benjamin Franklin, Thomas Edison or Alexander Graham Bell. Their determination changed the entire world. Their legacy is to have improved the lives of billions upon billions of people. Imagine being able to say that! Success requires focus. I focus on my little successes instead of my failures. Focusing on failure is really just a failure to focus. We all get knocked down, but we have to pick ourselves up and get back in the fight. I am not defined by my failures and neither are you.

I am sure you have heard the saying "Use it or lose it." How true it is! You have determination, imagination, confidence, self-esteem, joy, courage, faith, hope, curiosity, love, kindness, creativity, patience, compassion, honesty, cheerfulness and the ability to forgive. All of these are inside of you. Some might be buried under a ton of dirt, or afraid to peak their noses out and show themselves—but trust me, they are there. But you have to give each one of these characteristics the proper exercise or workout. Don't let these muscles get flabby from lack of use. If they're buried, dig down deep through the muck and pull them up onto the surface, into the light of day. If they're afraid to show themselves, give them a little prodding, or even a swift kick to the behind! That'll get them moving!

Wherever you invest your energy is where you will see returns. I actually think it takes more energy to complain than to be grateful. Negativity is heavy—it's a burden. Positivity is light—it's like helium, and lifts you off your feet. Negativity and positivity are both feedback loops. Putting either of these energies out there doesn't get rid of that energy. They're like boomerangs and come right back to the person who tossed them out into the world. Good brings good, bad brings bad, like brings like. If you're not paying attention, the boomerang will come back and hit you upside the head.

Have a good self-image. The better you think of yourself, the better your life will be. Don't be egotistical and go thinking you're the only awesome person who ever existed; but be confident that you are unique and have something unique to offer the world. The most important opinion we'll ever have will be the opinion we have of ourselves. You will be spending the rest of your life with yourself: try and make yourself somebody you want to spend time with. Your personal energy attracts similar energy. Downers attract downers, and people who get their jollies wallowing in the muck attract the same. Likewise, people who are up, enthusiastic, and optimistic attract the same. And when two or more people come together with that positive energy, beautiful things happen.

Have an attitude of gratitude. Life is an adventure. It can be a wild buck, but take it by the reins and hold on. Live this life! Contemplate the mystery and the miracle of existence. Don't take it for granted. There is nothing quite so amazing or startling as the mere fact that we are here, on a gorgeous planet, floating in space around an enormous star. When we keep in mind that the mere fact of our existence is spectacular, we easily come to see every day as a gift. And when we see every day as a rare and precious gift, we'll be motivated to make the most productive use of this gift.

Remember, sharing is caring. Being of service to others is always simultaneously a service to yourself. Try being selfless instead of selfish. Doing good and earning accolades for ourselves is certainly a thrill and a boost to our self-esteem. But quite honestly, it is nothing like the natural high we get from helping others achieve their goals, and inspiring them to go after their dreams. But we have to set the example. We have to live what we preach. Once we accomplish our goals, we have the ability to show others that it can really, truly be done.

Words shape us and seal our fate. The words you speak to yourself become self-fulfilling prophecies. Words attract energy. Don't let the "inner me" become the "enemy." Using the right language is the first step in forming the right frame of mind.

Once we shape our minds and our thoughts, our lives come to resemble our state of mind.

There is always a second chance. Just because you've had a few hard knocks doesn't mean the fight is over. You are still alive; this fact alone means there are more opportunities waiting for you. Just when you think you're onto life's boxing style, it will throw a loopy haymaker and set you off balance so it can deliver the one-two punch that knocks you to the canvas. But pick yourself off the mat and put your dukes up. There is always another round left, and you can still pull out a win.

Formulate a vision. Have goals and get ready to rock. Make use of your time instead of being used by it. Find purpose. If you have no purpose in life, you just bounce around in mediocrity. If you look around you and cannot find a purpose, try putting yourself in a new environment. New horizons force us to look at the world in a different way, and fresh ideas come from fresh surroundings.

160

Have fun. What good is making money if you don't know how to have any fun with it? Know how to laugh. A good, honest belly-laugh is more precious than gold. The days of our lives should not be filled with misery and grouchiness. A day without a laugh is a day that is wasted.

Vance Havner said it perfectly when he said, "Vision is not enough. It must be combined with venture. It is not enough to stare up the steps, we must step up the stairs."

Think of the first steps you are going to make. Step one is always believe in yourself. But it all starts with a goal. I write down my goals so that I can map out the means of getting there. It doesn't matter if it's a financial, physical, intellectual, or spiritual goal. Imagine what it feels like to have already achieved your goal. Get in commitment mode. How bad do you want to achieve the goal? What resources will you bring to bear in going after it? What sacrifices are you willing to make? If I am writing it down on paper, I am also writing it down in my head and imprinting it on my soul. I know I am fully committed. I will do whatever it takes to make the dream a reality.

Define your goals very clearly and precisely. It helps you map out and anticipate obstacles. It also helps you break the big goal down into smaller goals. Short-range goals are the stepping-stones on the way to achieving big things. Big goals don't get achieved overnight, but the little goals add up quickly, and when the big victory finally happens, it will feel like it happened overnight. My overnight success took almost sixteen years to accomplish, so I was not surprised when it happened. I'd spent every day of my life working towards it.

If it was easy, it wouldn't be worth it. Obstacles will come, oh yes they will. For me, working hard is a daily business. It is a marathon, not a sprint. "Success is not a result of luck. It is a result of how you spend your free time." I always have a few different goals, so that when I need a break from one I can focus on another. Very few painters work only on one piece at a time— they work on many. Put passion into all your actions, and have many actions devoted to different passions.

Tell yourself that you are going to have a life that counts. You are going to make an effort to never give up. You are full of determination. You are ready to work hard and play hard. You will be the master of your time. Let go of your mistakes; today is a new day. Be ground zero for an epidemic of positivity. You are going to be a doer and not a procrastinator. You are going to be a dreamer and not a dream-denier. You are going to hang out with others who lift you up and encourage your self-actualization. Shed your bad habits, and let good habits take root through repetition.

I can shout at you until I am blue in the face, but if you don't have the inner desire to say "I am doing this for me", then no amount of motivational speaking will light the spark.

Life is about making progress. People are going to try and talk you out of your dreams. They will suck up your time with nay-saying, or criticize you and pick you apart.

163

But you tell them that Derek said to back off. Stay away from those people who are imprisoned by negativity. They're not even doing good for themselves, so how can they possibly be doing good for you?

Don't worry about failing. It is nothing. It is the voice of other people ringing inside our heads. Failure is a great teacher and in a way has been my friend all along. Remember Thomas Edison's quote: "I have not failed. I've just found 10,000 ways that won't work." Failure is also a test. Failure might be telling us that we need to change direction and execute a different plan of attack or a new strategy.

To be successful, we must be strategic in taking risks. Risks will take us to untamed and uncharted territory, but it is in these places that we become all we can be.

Stay creative. Sometimes you will have to sit quiet for thirty minutes, so you can clear your mind of all the noise. You will be amazed at what ideas or revelations come to you when you just put aside all the distractions of modern life.

164

I hope that you are no longer afraid to envision a better future. I hope that you are ready to live life without limits. As long as you still have breath in your lungs, there is time to start over. As long as there is blood running in your veins, you have time to make your dreams happen. We have the rest of our lives from this moment on to realize our ambitions.

Change the world by changing yourself. Once you are confident about your own ability to achieve, you can help create a world of achievers through your example.

Never limit your life, and never give up!

Check Out Derek's Inspirational Corporate Keynote

Corporate Sales Motivation and Personal Development Training

Utilizing the Power of Attitude to Overcome Adversity Within Your Organization.

Reach New Heights With Your Organization!

An employee's peak performance is directly correlated to their attitude about overcoming adversity. Confidence in meeting unforeseen challenges is a turn of mind that is essential when confronting any problem, professional or personal. Companies and employees are both being tested by life's many hardships. However, with the right attitude, adversity is the spur to enrich us all and find success in any enterprise.

167

As the founder of several successful corporations, Derek knows that each member's leadership, teamwork, and motivational capabilities play critical roles in the success of the organization as a whole. When individuals push themselves beyond their limits, everyone around them grows in strength and character. Hope and positivity are not only contagious, but the keys to higher productivity. By cultivating drive, focus, and fearlessness, employees will find their professional and personal lives opening up to new promise and fresh opportunities.

Derek's programs inspire people to discover the resources within themselves to overcome any obstacle, no matter how daunting. Audiences nationwide have been inspired by his powerful message of hope, determination and courage. Combining his business expertise with a triumphant personal history, Derek has shown his listeners that they too can thrive in their organizations by reaching beyond self-imposed limitations. He has shown that everyone has the power to take leadership through personal accountability and vision.

Derek is an inspiring motivational speaker and author of the *I Will Never Give Up* book series. His corporate audiences will be ignited with the courage to take decisive action. They will learn the practical value of keeping the faith and never giving up. He will help them realize that all limitations are self-imposed. Employees will benefit from his powerful message of hope and unwavering perseverance. His true-life trials and personal triumphs will excite and motivate. He will demonstrate that personal and professional success begins, first and foremost, with our attitude.

Spend a day with Derek and start believing that there truly are NO LIMITS.

Contact: Derek Clark
Phone: 1-800-980-0751
Email: Seminars@NeverLimitYourLife.com

Websites: www.NeverLimitYourLife.com and www.IWillNeverGiveUp.com

CONTACT ME

You may contact Derek Clark at

Derek@NeverLimitYourLife.com

Visit Derek Clark's websites
www.NeverLimitYourLife.com
and
www.IWillNeverGiveUp.com

Derek Clark is an inspiring speaker whose message conveys a "realistic" mix of hope, encouragement and determination by sharing his sad and triumphant experiences. On stage, his passion for life and music will touch and warm the audience's soul. He brings humor and the power of music to inspire others change the direction of their life. They will walk away with a new focus and the confidence to overcome any obstacles in their life.

To have Derek Clark be part of your next event, email seminars@iwillnevergiveup.com

Derek would love to hear your story of overcoming adversity and how you Never Gave Up.

For more information on Derek's products and services, please visit his websites.

<u>Take a Shot of Power and Purpose</u>

Some Quotes That have Inspired Me

"Never tell me the sky's the limit when there are footprints on the moon." - Unknown

"Never quit....
Fight on my men, Sir Andrew says.
A little I'm hurt, but yet not slain;
I'll but lie down and bleed awhile,
and then I'll rise and fight again."
-- Ballad of Sir Andrew Barton

"Cherish your visions and your dreams. They are the children of your soul, the blueprints of your ultimate achievements." - Napoleon Hill

"Resolve to be a master of change rather than a victim of change." - Brian Tracy

"I know quite certainly that I myself have no special talent; curiosity, obsession and dogged endurance, combined with self-criticism, have brought me to my ideas." - Albert Einstein

"The person who goes farthest is generally the one who is willing to do and dare." - Dale Carnegie

"Buried deep within each of us is a spark of greatness, a spark than can be fanned into flames of passion and achievement. That spark is not outside of you it is born deep within you." - James A. Ray

"Never talk defeat. Use words like hope, belief, faith, victory." - Norman Vincent Peale

"The happiness of my life depends on the quality of my thoughts." – Unknown

"Although the world is full of suffering, it is also full of the overcoming of it." - Helen Keller

"As long as you think the problem is out there, that very thought is the problem." - Stephen Covey

"One thing I can't recycle is wasted time." – Unknown

"When I examine myself and my methods of thought, I come to the conclusion that the gift of fantasy has meant more to me than my

174

talent for absorbing positive knowledge." - Albert Einstein

"It is never too late to become what I might have been." - Unknown

"How far you go in life depends on you being tender with the young, compassionate with the aged, sympathetic with the striving and tolerant of the weak and the strong. Because someday in life you will have been all of these." - George Washington Carver

"If you aren't fired with enthusiasm, you'll be fired with enthusiasm." - Vince Lombardi

"I'm a great believer in luck, and I find the harder I work the more I have of it." - Thomas Jefferson

"Resolve says, 'I Will.' The man says, 'I will climb this mountain. They told me it is too high, too far, too steep, too rocky and too difficult. But it's my mountain. I will climb it. You will soon see me waving from the top or dead on the side from trying." - Jim Rohn

"What the mind of a man can conceive and believe, the mind of a man can achieve." - Napolean Hill

"Men are not prisoners of fate, but only prisoners of their own minds." - Franklin Delano Roosevelt

"You are today where your thoughts have brought you; you will be tomorrow where your thoughts take you." - James Allen

"Never let your memories be greater than your dreams." - Doug Ivester

"I have had dreams and I have had nightmares, but I have conquered my nightmares because of my dreams." - Dr.Jonas Salk

"You block your dream when you allow your fear to grow bigger than your faith." - Mary Manin Morrissey

"There is a time to take counsel of your fears, and there is a time to never listen to any fear." - George S. Patton

"To realize a dream, you must have a dream to realize." - Mark Victor Hansen

"The only limit to our realization of tomorrow will be our doubts of today." - Franklin Delano Roosevelt

"The most influential person who will talk to you all day is you, so you should be very careful about what you say to you!" - Zig Ziglar

"When you come to the edge of all the light you know, and are about to step off into the darkness of the unknown, faith is knowing one of two things will happen: there will be something solid to stand on, or you will be taught how to fly."
 - Barbara J. Winter